KU-215-194

ANGELS SURROUND US

Dedication

I dedicate this book to Sarah, my best friend and wife for over 25 years. Your editing skills were vitally important for accurately writing God's Word. Perhaps most importantly, Sarah thank you for your never-ending encouragement to wholeheartedly follow Christ which is a great daily source of joy. You are truly my angel sent from on high.

ANGELS SURROUND US

THE TRUTH ABOUT ANGELS AND FALLEN ANGELS

BY

EDWARD L. TAGGART

ISBN 1-85792-681-1

© Edward Taggart

Published in 2001
by
Christian Focus Publications Ltd.
Geanies House, Fearn, Tain,
Ross-shire, IV20 1TW, Great Britain
www.christianfocus.com

Printed and bound by
Guernsey Press, Guernsey

Cover Design by Alister MacInnes

Contents

PART 2

Foreword

Edward Taggart, a brilliant lawyer, has put his trained legal mind to use by writing a tremendous and extensive volume on the supernatural. This masterful work concerning angels documents practically every statement made about them in God's holy, inerrant Word. I highly recommend this inspiring work because Angelology is one of the most important subjects for the latter days. Here is why:

There's a war raging today that by comparison makes World Wars I and II look like school-yard brawls. Swords are clashing, nations are being lost and millions of lives hang in the balance. I'm talking about a vast and intense spiritual conflict in which planet earth has been a principal battlefield since the beginning of time. The key warriors in this intergalactic struggle are the Holy Trinity leading a heavenly host of hundreds of millions of faithful, supernatural, powerful, angelic beings battling Lucifer, once God's most perfect created being.

In Ephesians 6:12 we read, 'For we wrestle not against flesh and blood, but against principalities, against powers, against the rulers of the darkness of this world, against spiritual wickedness in high places.' These titles – principalities, powers and spirit wickedness in high places ... designate ranks of service similar to five-star generals, captains, lieutenants, right down to buck privates. Because Satan's angels can't be everywhere at all times, they must follow this chain of command to relay messages to their leaders. You see Satan is not omniscient like our God. He must have informants and agents to keep him posted on world events.

In some ways, angels resemble mankind – with free will, egos, pride and a bent toward temptation. But, in other ways, they are quite different. For one thing, their power is awesome. Entire cities have been wiped out by God's angels in the blink of an eye. One angel slew 185,000 people in one evening's work. Angels have power – and they can exercise it in the physical world. Judging from the sheer volume of references to angels in Scripture, these heavenly beings have played leading roles in history and will continue to do so in the future.

1 Thessalonians 4: 16-18 indicates that on the day of the Rapture, earthly believers will be swept up into the clouds to meet the Lord at the command of the archangel and the assistance of millions upon millions of angels. In fact, each of us could have an angel guide us in the presence of God. Remember angels transported Elijah home – an example of the coming Rapture (II Kings 2:11).

The final great role God's loyal angels play is undoubtedly the moment when Christ returns with His saints, and myriads of angels accompany Him from heaven. Matthew 25:31 says He will come in His glory with all His holy angels, and then He shall sit upon the throne of His glory here on earth. That will be the day all heaven and earth rejoices!

If these few facts have stirred your heart and peaked your interest, I know you will be tremendously blessed as you delve into literally hundreds of facts Edward Taggart has so masterfully presented for your edification.

Dr. Jack Van Impe, President
Jack Van Impe Ministries International

Introduction and Prayer

For this study of God's created angels I pray earnestly that the Word of God, by the power of the Holy Spirit, gives me wisdom to understand God's ways so as to glorify His name and the name of Christ Jesus my Lord, controlling my thoughts and mind so His pleasure is done. I have kept in the forefront of my mind during this study Proverbs 30:5-6: 'Every word of God is pure: he is a shield unto them that put their trust in him. Add thou not unto his words, lest he reprove thee, and thou be found a liar.'

Such a study as this will surely endure to anyone's righteousness as the pages of God's Word are turned back and forth and back again seeking answers by study. Psalms 119:9-16 speaks to such a study of His Word:

Wherewithall shall a young man cleanse his way? By taking heed thereto according to thy word. With my whole heart have I sought thee: O let me not wander from thy commandments. Thy word have I hid in mine heart, that I might not sin against thee. Blessed art thou, O Lord: teach me thy statutes. With my lips have I declared all the judgments of thy mouth. I have rejoiced in the way of thy testimonies, as much as in all riches. I will meditate in thy precepts, and have respect unto thy ways. I will delight myself in thy statutes: I will not forget thy word.

I thank God for the opportunity and inclination to study His Word while knowing that, 'Heaven and earth shall pass away, but my words shall not pass away' (Matt. 24:35). Praise God for the knowledge come real that, 'It is written, Man shall not live by bread alone, but by every word that proceedeth out of the mouth of God' (Matt. 4:4).

Falling to my knees with thanks for the plan of salvation by God the Father, God the Son and God the Spirit as expressed in John 1:1-4, 14:

In the beginning was the Word, and the Word was with God, and Word was God. The same was in the beginning with God. All things were made by him; and without him was not any thing made that was made. In him was life; and the life was in the light of men ... And the Word was made flesh, and dwelt among us, (and we beheld his glory, the glory as of the only begotten of the Father,) full of grace and truth.

After reading Scripture and what the Holy Spirit and Jesus have said therein we know that angels and demons exist and play a part in the lives of the people of this world. The references to these created beings are numerous and extend from near the beginning in Genesis to the end in Revelation. According to the Word of our Lord Jesus, angels are personal, sinless, immortal beings, existing in great number, and in close relation not only with individual men but also with the history of God's kingdom (Matt. 13:39; 18:10; 22:30; 25:31; 26:53; Luke 15:10; 16:22). His words concerning angels are true, and if spoken to us by our Lord clearly of value.

Scripture also teaches that Satan is called the 'ruler of the demons' (Matt. 9:34; 12:24; Mark 3:22; Luke 11:15; Gk. *archonti ton daimonion*).

To doubt whether angels are real is to doubt the Holy Word of God! 2 Timothy 3:16 teaches: 'All scripture comes from the inspiration of God, and is profitable for doctrine, for reproof, for correction, for instruction in righteousness: That the man of God may be perfect, thoroughly furnished unto all good works.' And, 2 Peter 1:20-21 explains: 'Knowing this first, that no prophecy of the scripture is of any private interpretation. For the prophecy came not in old time by the will of man: but holy men of God spake as they were moved by the Holy Ghost.' Paul reminds us 'whatsoever things were written aforetime were written for our learning, that we through patience and comfort of the scriptures might have hope' (Rom. 15:4).

This study depends upon Scripture for the truth of the information presented. If any question or concern arises about my personal interpretation or others cited please feel free to read the presented Scriptures and pray the Holy Spirit for interpretation. The denial of the existence of angels, including that of a personal devil and demons, exists because of an unholy, unbelieving spirit, which in its most terrible form denies the existence of God and His Word.

How to Read and Understand Scripture

Understanding Scripture Comes By Faith, Prayer, Obedience and Earnest Study

A degree in seminary is not necessary to understand the Word of God. Searching Scripture itself reveals the 'secrets' to understanding the meaning behind the stories and words. The 'secrets' are simple principles which must be respected before the Holy Spirit will help us to understand the meaning and purpose of the Holy Word of God.

No one can fully understand the Word until they die to this world and are reborn in the Spirit. In other words, reading the Bible with preconceived ideas about its reliability or accuracy, at all doubting the infallibility of the Bible as the inspired Word of God, will result in confusion and misunderstanding, no matter how much time you spend reading or studying.

'If God be for us, who can be against us? He that spared not his own Son, but delivered him up for us all, how shall he not with him also freely give us all things?' (Rom. 8:31-32). Yes, trust in God's plan of salvation by believing that His Son Jesus died on the cross for our sins and was raised alive for our redemption: then you shall be reborn in the Spirit of God, meaning forevermore that God will be for you and freely give you understanding of His Word by the Holy Spirit who will dwell in you (Rom. 8:1-11).

'All scripture is given by inspiration of God' (2 Tim. 3:16). Yes, all of the Bible is inspired. 'Inspiration' comes from the Greek word *theopneustos*, a combination of two words: *theos*, from which we get 'theistic' (the Word of God), and *pneuma*, from which we get 'pneumatic', having to do with air or wind or breath. Thus, inspiration literally means 'God-breathed'. Another legitimate translation of this Scripture in 2 Timothy would be 'all Scripture is God-breathed (or expired by God)'. John Calvin said that, 'Every word of Scripture is to be taken as if it dripped from the lips of the Almighty; it is the very Word of God.'

Faith in the truth of the Word is required because Hebrews 11:3 teaches us, 'through faith we understand that the worlds were framed by the word of God, so that things which are seen were not made of things which do appear.' 'Now faith is the substance of things hoped for, the evidence of things not seen. For by it the elders obtained a good report' (Heb. 11:1-2). A good report by our trust and faith before God should be our daily striving goal. 'Without faith it is impossible to please Him, for he who comes to God must believe that He is, and that He is a rewarder of those who diligently seek Him' (Heb. 11:6). Jesus teaches us to have faith in the truth of all Scripture when He teaches: 'Not one jot or tittle shall in any wise pass from the law till all be fulfilled' (Matt. 5:18). A 'jot' is the smallest letter in the Hebrew alphabet and a 'tittle' is simply a curly cue on the end of various letters. God's inspiration deals with the minutest details and not even a Word or a letter or even a tiny part of a letter will pass away, according to Jesus.

We should spend time in earnest prayer before reading Scripture. We are told in Psalm 119:18-19: 'Open my eyes, that I may behold wondrous things out of thy law. I am a stranger in the earth: hide not thy commandments from me.' If you truly want your eyes opened to the spiritual things of God pray this prayer. 'Let my cry come before You, O Lord; Give me understanding according to Your word' (Ps. 119:169). 'And this is the confidence that we have in him, that, if we ask any thing according to his will, he heareth us: and if we know that he hear us, whatsoever we ask, we know that we have the petitions that we desired of him' (1 John 5:14-15). Truly God's will is that we seek Him by reading and understanding His Holy Scripture.

'But the wisdom that is from above is first pure' (Jas. 3:17). When there is sin in our hearts that remains unconfessed and unforsaken, it presents a barrier to our ability to interpret the Bible. Seeking purity of heart and thought is essential for knowing the wisdom of God and being able to understand Scripture. By seeking moral purity we will live a clean life according to God. 'If I regard iniquity in my heart, the Lord will not hear' (Ps. 66:18). Morality, purity of heart and clean living are clearly implied by Peter when he says: 'Therefore, laying aside all malice, all guile, hypocrisy, envy, and all evil speaking, as newborn babes, desire the pure milk of the word, that you may grow thereby, if indeed you have tasted that the Lord is gracious' (1 Pet. 2:1-3).

Obedience to the Word as you do your reading is important to understanding. 'I understand more than the ancients, because I keep thy precepts' (Ps. 119:100). Through obedience you must truly seek to know God's will. Jesus teaches: 'If anyone wants to do His [God's] will, he shall know concerning the doctrine, whether it is from God or whether I speak on my own authority' (John 7:17). Thirsting for and keeping the Word in our heart and on our lips cleanses us; our very souls our cleansed. 'Thy word have I hid in mine heart, that I might not sin against thee' (Ps. 119:11). 'Make me understand the way of thy precepts: so shall I talk of thy wondrous works' (Ps. 119:27).

Finally, you must spend your time often, making a real effort, studying the Bible to understand God's Word. It takes time, patience and effort. We can all take to heart the encouragement to the believers at Berea: 'These were more fair-minded than those in Thessalonica, in that they received the word with all readiness, and searched the Scriptures daily to find out whether these things were so' (Acts 17:11). 'Blessed are they that keep His testimonies, and that seek Him with the whole heart' (Ps. 119:2).

All too often people simply make a cursory reading of a verse or part of a verse before giving up, complaining the Bible is confusing or too complicated. These people all too often give up and rely upon their pastor or minister as the final authority, instead of seeking and trusting the 'still small voice' of God as He speaks to them by the Holy Spirit. You must take time to actually search the Scriptures, not just read a verse here or there. Timothy is taught an invaluable lesson from Paul: 'Be diligent to present yourself approved to God, a worker who does not need to be ashamed, rightly dividing the word of truth' (2 Tim. 2:15).

Once you begin reading the Bible with the foundation of faith, praying for understanding, living as the Word teaches and repenting of sin, seeking always to stay pure and obedient to the commands of the Word, you will be shown by the Holy Spirit that the entire Bible is infallible and inerrant – without error. Throughout the Bible we read that: 'God spake all these words, saying...' God spake through men inspired by His Spirit. We should honour God by trusting His Word: 'Whoso despiseth the word shall be destroyed' (Prov. 13:13). Based upon this Scripture, the question you need to ask yourself is what your attitude is toward the Word of God because your attitude determines God's attitude toward you. If we seek Him we will find Him. If we honour Him, He will honour us. If we honour His Word He will honour our prayers. And, if we trust in Jesus Christ we become adopted sons and daughters and may claim the message to all of God's chosen people of assured victory over the enemies of God and His children: '[The Spirit of the Lord] said, Hearken ye ... Thus saith the Lord unto you, Be not afraid nor dismayed by reason of this great multitude; for the battle is not yours, but God's. Tomorrow go ye down against [the enemy]... Ye shall not need to fight in this battle: set yourselves, stand ye still, and see the salvation of the Lord with you, ... fear not, nor be dismayed; tomorrow go out against them: for the Lord will be with you' (2 Chron. 20:15-17).

Correct interpretation of God's Word begins with your relationship with Christ Jesus as your personal Lord and Saviour, then earnest prayer, with a repentant heart seeking to live morally and purely, diligently studying and searching Scripture for its inerrant truths. *On your day of judgment before Jesus, what will your answer be to His question: 'How did you like my book?'* One day my wife asked me just that question and my answer at the time left me ashamed. Please do not be ashamed at your face-to-face encounter with Jesus; it could be tomorrow or in fifty years, but none of us is promised tomorrow.

I hope this study on angels helps you to understand God's plan of salvation and His assurances to us as believers in His Son, that God the Father, Son and Holy Spirit and their ministering angels who are with us are greater than he who is in the world.

PART 1

Chapter 1

The Truth about Angels According to God's Word

Three Foundational Definitions

Angels: (Heb. *mal'ak*; Gk. *angelos*, both meaning 'messenger'). In some cases the word may be applied to human beings (Mal. 2:7: preacher as messenger of Lord; Rev. 1:20: seven stars of the church may be angels or church leaders) or even figuratively to impersonal agents (Exod. 14:19; 2 Sam. 24:16-17; Ps. 104:4). Spiritual and superhuman beings are who are most commonly spoken of in Scripture. However, even in the listed Scriptures the word angels can legitimately be translated as God's holy angels, except for Malachi who clearly is a human preacher. Only a few books do not mention angels: Ruth, Nehemiah, Esther, the epistles of John and James.

Daystar: (Gk. *phosphorus*, 'light-bearing'; Lat. *Lucifer*). The KJV rendering of 'morning star', the planet Venus (2 Pet. 1:19). The meaning of the passage is that the prophets were like a lamp, but Christ Himself is the light of dawn, heralded as the 'the bright and morning star' (Rev. 22:16).

Christ: (Gk. *Christos*, 'anointed', from the Greek for the Hebrew *Meshiah* (Messiah), meaning 'anointed one'). The official title of our Saviour who was consecrated (anointed) by His baptism by John and the descent of the Holy Spirit as our Prophet, High Priest, King of Kings and Lord of Lords. (Heb. word for anointing is *mashah*; the Gk. term is *chrisma* meaning 'ointment' or, *chrio*, to 'rub' or 'smear'). Jacob anointed (consecrated) the stone, or spot, for a sacred purpose (Gen. 28:18; 35:14). The anointing of the Holy Spirit upon believers of Jesus (1 John 2:20) was an aid in receiving comfort and understanding the truth Scripture teaches (John 16:12-15) and thus to glorify Jesus

(John 16:14) in whom the full revelation of God had been given (John 16:15).

Jesus started His ministry by proclaiming in the synagogue at Nazareth: *'The Spirit of the Lord God is upon me; because the Lord hath anointed me to preach the gospel* to the poor; he hath sent me to heal the brokenhearted, to preach deliverance to the captives, and recovery of sight to the blind, to set at liberty them that are bruised, To preach the acceptable year of the Lord... This day is this scripture fulfilled in your ears' (Luke 4:18-19, 21; see Is. 61:1-2).

Chapter 2

Angels Speak for the Glory of Thy Name

Angels speak from heaven for the glory of the Father. Jesus rode on a young ass into Jerusalem and many people took branches of palm trees, went forth to meet him, and cried, 'Hosanna: Blessed is the King of Israel that cometh in the name of the Lord' (John 12:13-14). Then Jesus spoke:

> The hour is come, that the Son of man should be glorified.
>
> Verily, verily, I say unto you, Except a corn of wheat fall into the ground and die, it abideth alone: but if it die, it bringeth forth much fruit.
>
> He that loveth his life shall lose it; and he that hateth his life in this world shall keep it unto life eternal.
>
> If any man serve me, let him follow me; and where I am, there shall also my servant be: if any man serve me, him will my Father honour.
>
> Now is my soul troubled; and what shall I say? Father, save me from this hour: but for this cause came I unto this hour.
>
> Father, glorify thy name.
>
> (John 12:23-28).

The function of angels to glorify the name of God the Father is exemplified where Jesus responds to an angel of the Lord who speaks from heaven so as to glorify the Father's name. The Scripture records that the angel's voice thundered from heaven 'saying, I have both glorified it, and will glorify it again' (John 12:28-29). Truly, 'it' is the Father's name which is being glorified! The angels and Jesus have as a primary goal to glorify the Father's name. To make the point abundantly clear Jesus explains: 'This voice came not because of me, but for your sakes' (John 12:30). Jesus completely understands His purpose of glorifying the Father's name and He wants to be assured we also understand the purpose of his life, death and resurrection. Jesus tells the world that: 'He that believeth on me, believeth not on me, but on him that sent me. And he that seeth me seeth him that sent me' (John 12:44-45).

Why did the shepherds run to Bethlehem to find Mary and the new-born Messiah who was laying in a manger? And, why did they leave to share their find with many others before returning to the manger for the purpose of 'glorifying and praising God for all the things that they had heard and seen, as it was told to them'? (Luke 2:15-20). Let us look to see what the angel of the Lord said to them:

> And, lo, the angel of the Lord came upon them, and the glory of the Lord shone round about them: and they were sore afraid. And the angel said unto them, Fear not: for, behold, I bring you good tidings of great joy, which shall be to all people.
>
> For unto you is born this day in the city of David a Saviour, which is Christ the Lord. And this shall be a sign unto you; Ye shall find the babe wrapped in swaddling clothes, lying in a manger.
>
> And suddenly there was with the angel a multitude of the heavenly host praising God, and saying, Glory to God in the highest, and on earth peace, and good will toward men.
>
> And it came to pass, as the angels were gone away from them into heaven, the shepherds said one to another, Let us now go even unto Bethlehem, and see this thing which is come to pass, which the Lord hath made known unto us (Luke 2:9-15).

The prophet Isaiah explains perfectly why the shepherds ran to the people to explain what they had seen and heard and why they returned to the manger so they could continue 'glorifying and praising God for all the things that they had heard and seen': *The people that walked in darkness have seen a great light: they that dwell in the land of the shadow of death, upon them hath the light shined'* (Is. 9:2). Isaiah continues to explain what form of light the shepherds would see and exalt: *'For unto us a child is born, unto us a son is given: and the government shall be upon his shoulder: and his name shall be called Wonderful, Counsellor, The mighty God, The everlasting Father, The Prince of Peace'* (Is. 9:6). And if these shepherds knew of the revelation of the coming Messiah they would have understood the everlasting effect of this child's birth: *'Of the increase of his government and peace there shall be no end, upon the throne of David, and upon his kingdom, to order it, and to establish it with judgment and with justice from henceforth even for ever. The zeal of the Lord of hosts will perform this'* (Is. 9:7). Glory to God the Father, Son and Holy Spirit; and, praise to the Lord of hosts for His undying zeal.

Chapter 3

When and Where did Angels Come From?

The angels were created prior to God's creation of the earth (Job 38:7). Angels are called 'sons of God' while Lucifer is called by this name or by one of his many other names such as, Satan, Devil, Enemy, Great red dragon (destructive creature), Evil one, Roaring lion, Murderer or god of this world. Job 1:6 and 2:1 describe these 'sons of God' coming and presenting themselves before the Lord; Satan came also among these angels to present himself before the Lord. (See also Job 38:7). Satan, himself being an angelic being, joined the other created angels on these occasions.

All of the angels were instantly created. Scripture tells us many things about angels, but whether they were created at the same time by God is unclear. 'All things were made by him (Jesus); and without him was not any thing made that was made' (John 1:3). Everything that is created by the Lord is commanded to praise Him:

> Praise ye the Lord. Praise ye the Lord from the heavens: praise him in the heights.
> Praise ye him, all his angels: praise ye him, all his hosts.
> Praise ye him, sun and moon: praise him, all ye stars of light.
> Praise him, ye heavens of heavens, and ye waters that be above the heavens.
> Let them praise the name of the Lord: *for he commanded, and they were created* (Ps. 148:1-5).

Angels are created beings

Angels, like men, are created beings. As such, at one time they did not exist. 'Thou are worthy, O Lord, to receive glory and honour and power: for thou hast created all things, and for thy pleasure they are and were created' (Rev. 4:11). Angels have no power to create other living creatures. Scripture teaches that all things in heaven and earth were created by the Triune God: Father, Son and Holy Spirit. 'For it pleased the Father that in him [Jesus Christ] should all fulness dwell... Who is the image of the invisible God, the firstborn of every creature: For by him were all things created, that are in heaven, and that are in earth, visible and invisible, whether they be thrones, or dominions, or principalities, or powers: all things were created by him, and for him: And he is before all things, and by him all things consist' (Col. 1:19, 15-17).

Everything we see and rely upon in the physical remains (continues to exist) and would cease to exist if it pleased Jesus. This is what is meant by 'and by him all things consist' (Col. 1:17). Our modern scientists call what holds all unseen matter together at the atomic level as 'atomic glue'. Today's science has no idea exactly why all of the atomic substructure remains together and does not separate into complete chaos! Angelic beings, as heavenly spirits, understand their continued existence depends upon the grace of Jesus. Elihu in the book of Job reminds us: 'If he set his heart upon man, *if* he gather unto himself his spirit and his breath; All flesh shall perish together, and man shall turn again into dust' (Job 34:14-15).

Angels have ordered positions to glorify God

Angels come in various varieties and forms. They have different authority. Michael is the only named archangel in the Bible. An angel of the Lord named Gabriel on four occasions is God's messenger of very good news. The Bible also describes seraphim and cherubim angels.

Seraphim Angels

Seraphim comes from either the Hebrew root word, '*sarap*', meaning either 'love' or 'burning ones' or 'nobles' or an Arab term '*shrafa*' signifying 'high' or 'exalted'. Scripture speaks about seraphim angels on one occasion where Isaiah says:

> I saw also the Lord sitting upon a throne, high and lifted up, and his train filled the temple.

Above it stood the seraphims: each one had six wings; with twain [two] he covered his face, and with twain he covered his feet, and with twain he did fly.
And one cried unto another, and said, Holy, holy, holy, is the Lord of hosts: the whole earth is full of his glory.
And the posts of the door moved at the voice of him that cried, and the house was filled with smoke.
Then said I, Woe is me! for I am undone; because I am a man of unclean lips, and I dwell in the midst of a people of unclean lips: for mine eyes have seen the King, the Lord of hosts.
Then flew one of the seraphims unto me, having a live coal in his hand, which he had taken with the tongs from off the altar:
And he laid it upon my mouth, and said, Lo, this hath touched thy lips; and thine iniquity is taken away, and thy sin purged (Is. 6:1-7).

God placed seraphim angels above his throne as they exalted His glory by crying out to each other: 'Holy, holy, holy is the Lord of hosts: the whole earth is full of his glory.' The seraphim angels' voices are so powerful their cries of worship cause the posts of the door to be moved and the house to be filled with smoke. As Isaiah experienced this expression of exaltation and saw 'the King, the Lord of hosts' he realized how unclean he was and the other people with whom he lived with because of their 'unclean lips'. Understanding the words of Isaiah as he cried out his woe, a seraphim flew to him to cleanse him and take away all iniquity and sin; the angel was able to cleanse Isaiah by taking 'a live coal in his hand, which he had taken ... from off the altar' and laying it upon Isaiah's lips. Do not believe anyone who down-plays the importance of your words; Yes, the speech from our lips is very important to God.

Four seraphim angels are vividly described glorifying God on His throne in Jesus' revelation to St. John:

[R]ound about the throne, were four beasts full of eyes before and behind.
And the first beast was like a lion, and the second beast like a calf, and the third beast had a face as a man, and the fourth beast was like a flying eagle.

And the four beasts had each of them six wings about him; and they were full of eyes within: and they rest not day and night, saying, Holy, holy, holy, Lord God Almighty, which was, and is to come (Rev. 4:6-8)

Interestingly, many who have prayed long and earnestly for biblical understanding have found similarity between Revelation's four living ones (or 'beasts' or angels) and the four Gospels' presentation of Jesus: (1) He is the Lion of the Tribe of Judah in Matthew (Matt. 1:1, 6, see also Gen. 49:9-10; Rev. 5:5); (2) He is the servant who became the sacrifice for sin in Mark (Mark 10:44-45; see Heb. 9:12, 19 describes the calf as a sacrificial animal); (3) He is the Son of man in Luke (Jesus identified himself as: 'That the Son of man is Lord also of the sabbath'); and, (4) He is linked to heaven like a flying eagle in John: 'Hereafter ye shall see heaven open, and the angels of God ascending and descending upon the Son of Man' (John 1:51). For further understanding of this comparison of how Jesus is presented in the Gospels I suggest you pray, always remembering God is listening. *Recall, that the 'golden vials full of odours, which are the prayer of saints' are near God at the time when the Lamb of God opens the 'sealed book' while at the throne of God* (Rev. 5:8).

We can glean that seraphim angels are burning in their hearts with love to constantly glorify God and they will, when directed to do so by God, cleanse and purify God's servants. Picture in your mind these glorious creatures hovering with wings swirling in a blur, as a hummingbird might hover, high and exalted above the throne of God while they constantly and powerfully cry out worship for our Holy God.

Cherubim angels: 'Living Creatures' and 'Wheels'

The glory of God is located above the cherubim angels (Ezek. 11:22). Scripture identifies the cherubim angel as also being called 'the living creature': 'This is the living creature that I saw under the God of Israel by the river of Chebar; and I knew that they were the cherubims. Every one had four faces apiece, and every one four wings; and the likeness of the hands of a man was under their wings' (Ezek. 10:20-21).

Ezekiel describes his first sight of these living creatures (which later he identifies as cherubim angels) as a 'whirlwind came out of the north, a great cloud, and a fire infolding itself, and a brightness was about it, and out of the midst thereof as the colour of amber, out of the midst of the fire. Also out of the midst thereof came the likeness of four living creatures' (Ezek. 1:4-5). 'The spirit of the living creature was in the wheels' (Ezek. 1:21). The description Ezekiel gives is remarkable, yet detailed; he says of the appearance of the four beings he saw:

They had the likeness of a man. And every one had four faces, and every one had four wings.

And their feet were straight feet; and the sole of their feet was like the sole of a calf's foot: and they sparkled like the colour of burnished brass.

And they had the hands of a man under their wings on their four sides; and they four had their faces and their wings.

Their wings were joined one to another; they turned not when they went; they went every one straight forward.

As for the likeness of their faces, they four had the face of a man, and the face of a lion, ... and the face of an ox [Ezekiel later realizes the ox face is the face of a cherubim (Ezek. 10:14, 22)]; ... [and] the face of an eagle.

... their wings were stretched upward; two wings of every one were joined one to another, and two covered their bodies (Ezek. 1:5-11).

As for the likeness of the living creatures, their appearance was like burning coals of fire, and like the appearance of lamps: it went up and down among the living creatures; and the fire was bright, and out of the fire went forth lightning (Ezek. 1:13).

As for their rings, they were so high that they were dreadful; and their rings were full of eyes round about them four (Ezek. 1:18).

Whithersoever the spirit was to go, they went, thither was their spirit to go; and the wheels were lifted up over against them: for the spirit of the living creature was in the wheels.

When those went, these went; and when those stood, these stood; and when those were lifted up from the earth, the wheels were lifted up over against them: for the spirit of the living creature was in the wheels (Ezek. 1:20-21).

The Spirit of God and the visible glory of the Lord as a man here described within the cherubim angels

Notice that wherever the 'spirit' went the cherubim / living creatures / wheels went because 'the spirit of the living creature was in the wheels' (Ezek. 1:20); The spirit is identified as God Himself by Ezekiel when he says 'the spirit entered into me when He spake unto me, and [the Spirit] set me upon my feet'; Ezekiel then was told by the spirit about the 'rebellious nation' and being told 'thou shalt speak my [God's] words unto them' (Ezek. 1:28; 2:2, 3, 7).

At least on this occasion, God's Spirit travels with and/or within the cherubims who are called living creatures and wheels (Ezek. 1:12). *And [God] rode upon a cherub, and did fly: and he was seen upon the wings of the wind*' (2 Sam. 22:11). Ezekiel provides a most beautiful and exhilarating picture of God's Spirit and how the Lord's hand protects His prophet:

> *Then the spirit took me up, and I heard behind me a voice of a great rushing, saying, Blessed be the glory of the Lord from his place.*
>
> I heard also the noise of the wings of the living creatures that touched one another, and the noise of the wheels over against them, and a noise of a great rushing.
>
> *So the spirit lifted me up,* and took me away, and I went in bitterness, in the heat of my spirit; *but the hand of the Lord was strong upon me* (Ezek. 3:12-14).

Where the voice of God is we can trust the Spirit of God is: 'I heard the noise of their wings, like the noise of great waters, *as the voice of the Almighty, the voice of speech,* as the noise of an host' (Ezek. 1:24).

Accompanying the cherubim angels at the throne of God were 'the living creature' which is referred to as the 'wheel' (Ezek. 10:13, 1:15). Actually, the 'wheel' is the same as the cherubim which is the same as the living creature. *And when the living creatures went, the wheels went by them: and when the living creatures were lifted up from the earth, the wheels were lifted up.* Whithersoever the spirit was to go, they went, *thither was their spirit to go ... for the spirit of the living creature was in the wheels'* (Ezek. 1:19-20).

Cherubim angels propelled by wings and wheels

The living creature cherubims, with their four faces, moved through space 'straight forward' even though they had 'wheels' moving about them. Below is a multi-sensed description of the cherubim when travelling upon the earth (Ezek. 1:15).

> They went every one straight forward: whither the spirit was to go, they went; and they turned not when they went (Ezek. 1:12).
> The appearance of the wheels and their work was like unto the colour of a beryl [blue green or turquoise]: and they four had one likeness: and their appearance and their work was as it were a wheel in the middle of a wheel (Ezek. 1:16).
> When they went, they went upon their four sides: and they turned not when they went.
> As for their rings, they were so high that they were dreadful; and their wings were full of eyes round about them four (Ezek. 1:17-18).

> And the likeness of the firmament [a solid expanse] upon the heads of the living creature was as the colour of the terrible crystal [or like ice], stretched forth over their heads above.
> And under the firmament were their wings straight, the one toward the other; every one had two, which covered on this side, and every one had two, which covered on that side, their bodies.
> And when they went, I heard the noise of their wings, like the noise of great waters, as the voice of the Almighty, the voice of speech, as the noise of an host ... (Ezek. 1:22-24).

The visible glory of the Lord seen as a man upon a dark richly blue throne located above the cherubim angels

After travelling the cherubim angels stopped. As they stood Ezekiel was able to see above the angels the likeness of a man on a throne which likeness was 'of the glory of the Lord' (Ezek. 1:26, 28). (Was this likeness the visible Man-God Christ Jesus?)

> And there was a voice from the firmament that was over their heads, when they stood, and had let down their wings.
>
> And above the firmament that was over their heads was the likeness of a throne, as the appearance of a sapphire stone [dark richly blue]: and *upon the likeness of the throne was the likeness as the appearance of a man above upon it.*
>
> And I saw as the colour of amber, as the appearance of fire round about within it, from the appearance of his loins even upward, and from the appearance of his loins downward, I saw as it were the appearance of fire, and it had brightness round about.
>
> As the appearance of the bow that is in the cloud in the day of rain, so was the appearance of the brightness round about. *This was the appearance of the likeness of the glory of the Lord* (Ezek. 1:25-28).

Cherubim angels constantly glorify God, as do seraphim angels. Cherubim angels desire greatly that God's glory will be spread across the earth to all nations: 'thou that dwellest between the cherubims, shine forth' (Ps. 80:1). As His people, our goal should be for His message of forgiveness to shine forth to all peoples. 'The Lord reigneth; let the people tremble: he sitteth between the cherubims; let the earth be moved' (Ps. 99:1). Scripture directs us to seek God's powerful influence: 'Turn us again, O God, and cause thy face to shine; and we shall be saved' (Ps. 80:3).

Cherubim are of a high order of angels

Cherubim angels receive the most important positions and tasks for glorifying God. Lucifer was described as the highest order of angels and created as a cherubim angel (Ezek. 28:14-15).

Cherubim angels are first introduced in Scripture guarding the way to the tree of life, insuring with the drawn swords the continued expulsion of Adam and Eve from paradise (Gen. 3:24). We are introduced in the Bible to two golden cherubim angel figures with their wings outstretched forming a covering shadow attached to the

Ark facing each other above the Mercy Seat (Exod. 25:18-20). We are also told that upon the Tabernacle's inward curtain and veil were embroidered cherubim angels (Exod. 26:1, 31; 36:8). In Hebrews we find that this order of angels is honoured as 'the cherubims of glory' (Heb. 9:5).

Scripture further speaks of David's honour to God while describing His mighty works, including creation of the heavens; David continues with: 'who maketh the clouds his chariot: who walketh upon the wings of the wind: Who maketh his angels spirits; his ministers a flaming fire' (Ps. 104:1-4). David honours the Lord for His intervention during battle against the Philistines where David's nephew slew one of the Philistine giants with six fingers and six toes. This giant who was killed was of the same family of giants in Gath who was slain earlier by David (2 Sam. 21:20-22). David then praises God who intervened in this battle against the Philistines by saying: 'And [God] rode upon a cherub, and did fly: and he was seen upon the wings of the wind' (2 Sam. 22:11).

With covering wings cherubims are watching God's mercy

The cherubim watched the worthy sacrifice of God's only begotten Son which is symbolized through the sprinkling of blood by the Israelite high priest upon the Mercy Seat of the Ark, a representation of the perfect maintenance of God's righteousness and love by the sacrifice of Jesus the Christ (Exod. 25:17-20; Rom. 3:24-26). The angelic hosts stand with wings outstretched covering the loving Sacrifice of our salvation made real through hearing the Word, then trusting the One who not only covers all our sins, but, actually condemns all our sin (Rom. 8:2-3). Moreover he cleanses us as holy heirs by His justification through our belief in His blood, thus making us adopted sons and daughters of God (Rom. 3: 23-26; 4:3-5; 8:31-39). *The cherubim worship through their covering wings while Jesus teaches: 'I am the way, the truth, and the life'* (John 14:6).

Is not the joyful cry of David familiar to many? 'The Lord is my rock, and my fortress, and my deliverer; ... in him will I trust: he is my shield, and the horn of my salvation, my high tower, and my refuge, my saviour; thou savest me from violence. I will call on the Lord, who is worthy to be praised: so shall I be saved from mine enemies' (2 Sam. 22:2-4).

'For God so loved the world, that he gave his only begotten Son, that whosoever believeth in him should not perish, but have everlasting life' (John 3:16). We are commanded to love God with all our heart, soul and mind, and to love our neighbour as ourselves (Mark 12:29-31). Jesus is perceived to love His Father 'because he laid down his life for us: and we ought to lay down our lives for the brethren' (1 John 3:16). 'How can ye believe, which receive honour one of another, and seek not the honour that cometh from God [the Father] only?' (John 5:44).

Thank God continually because He promises through faith in His Son our prayers will be answered: 'Ask, and it shall be given you; seek, and ye shall find; knock, and it shall be opened unto you: For every one that asketh receiveth; and he that seeketh findeth; and to him that knocketh it shall be opened' (Matt. 7:7-8). Jesus desires to proclaim to you: 'Son, be of good cheer; thy sins be forgiven thee' (Matt. 9:2). Angels witness the answer to your prayers for salvation. The two cherubim angels facing each other will surely smile and rejoice while hovering over the Mercy Seat of God and watching you receive your salvation through faith.

Anyone who has repented of sin and trusted Christ as Saviour will not be denied access by the cherubim angels to the inner sanctuary of God's throne. The veil in the temple was rent (torn open) allowing us open access to God's throne by Jesus' death on the cross. 'Jesus, when he had cried again with a loud voice, yielded up the ghost. And, behold, the veil of the temple was rent [torn] in twain from the top to the bottom; and the earth did quake, and the rocks rent' (Matt. 27:50-51). 'For through [Jesus] we both have access by one Spirit unto the Father. Now therefore ye are no more strangers and foreigners, but fellow citizens with the saints, and of the household of God' (Eph. 2:18-19).

Peter also assures us: 'But ye are a chosen generation, a royal priesthood, an holy nation, a peculiar people; that ye should shew forth the praises of him who hath called you out of darkness into his marvellous light: Which in time past were not a people, but are now the people of God: which had not obtained mercy, but now have obtained mercy' (1 Pet. 2:9-10). The cherubim only guard God's holy place from those who have no right of access. Believers in Jesus, through His redemptive work on the cross, now have direct access to the presence of God. We have become priests of God by our trust in Christ, assured of God's eternal mercy.

Created beings are not to be worshipped

Even though angels are mighty beings, and when they do appear they can be awe inspiring, we must be vigilant never to worship the messengers of God. Remember the First Commandment: 'Thou shalt have no other gods before me' (Exod. 20:3). 'Let no man beguile you of your reward in a voluntary humility and worshipping of angels, intruding into those things which he hath not seen, vainly puffed up by his fleshly mind' (Col. 2:18).

We can honestly say that the Israelites in the desert were not filled with the Spirit of God and failed to inwardly glorify Him. May we always pray for God's power to daily seek His face: 'Speaking to yourselves in psalms and hymns and spiritual songs, singing and making melody in your heart to the Lord; Giving thanks always for all things unto God and the Father in the name of our Lord Jesus Christ; Submitting yourselves one to another in the fear of God' (Eph. 5:19-21). The Israelites failed to give thanks for the peace of God which should have ruled their hearts (Col. 3:15).

Jesus teaches all of us how to pray and to whom we should pray: 'Our Father which art in heaven, Hallowed be thy name ...' (Matt. 6:9). Our prayers are heard by the Lord as the Psalmist states: 'The eyes of the Lord are upon the righteous, and his ears are open unto their cry... The righteous cry, and the Lord heareth, and delivereth them out of all their troubles' (Ps. 34:15, 17). On occasion angels may carry the answer to our prayers. The Scripture tells us that Daniel's righteous prayers for understanding were heard immediately by God; we also learn Gabriel was sent by God immediately to answer the prayers of Daniel. But, Gabriel was delayed with God's answer for twenty-one days by the Prince of Persia until Michael came to help (Dan. 10:13). However, it is clear to whom we should direct our prayers and praise: 'Praise waiteth for thee, O God, in Sion: and unto thee shall the vow be performed. O thou that hearest prayer, unto thee shall all flesh come' (Ps. 65:1-2).

Chapter 4

Vast Numbers of Angels Protect the Mount of God

In Scripture God's residence or home is identified as His 'Mount'. Holy angels always surround God. Seraphim angels hover above His throne worshipping Him and are vigilant to assure the purity of all coming near (Is. 6:1-7). Cherubim angels surround His throne glorifying Him (Heb. 9:5) and awaiting to do His commands (Ps. 104:1-4). God's holy angels are His 'ministers a flaming fire' (Ps. 104:1-4). God comes riding upon a cherub flying 'upon the wind' (2 Sam. 22:11). He comes as a 'whirlwind' of 'great cloud' and 'fire infolding itself' surrounded in utter 'brightness' (Ezek. 1:4-5). Also in the midst of the cloud of infolding fire are the living creatures which are the cherubim angels. (Ezek. 1:5). As God rides upon the wind He travels within the clouds of angels (Ezek. 1:28).

The Mount of God is holy and cannot be touched by any unholy being without suffering sure death. The angels of God are commanded to stone or impale with a lance any man or beast who would dare touch His mount. We first find the description of the warning about being killed for touching the Mount of God at Mount Sinai in Exodus where God speaks to Moses saying: 'There shall not an hand touch it, but he shall surely be stoned, or shot through; whether it be beast or man, it shall not live' (Exod. 19:13). God's holy angels were prepared to carry-out the commands of God as they always surround God. St. John hears the thunderous angel voices worshipping God: 'Worthy is the Lamb' with the numbers being at 'ten thousand times ten thousand, and thousands of thousands' (Rev. 5:11-12).

The Lord 'descended upon [Mount Sinai] in fire: and the smoke thereof ascended as the smoke of a furnace, and the whole mount quaked greatly. And the Lord came down upon mount Sinai, on the top of the mount: and the Lord called Moses up to the top of the mount...' (Exod. 19:18, 20). Ten thousands of angels came down on Mount Sinai to proclaim the presence of the holy God whom 'from his right hand went a fiery law for them [the children of Israel]' (Deut. 33:1-2). This scene, which led to God writing the ten commandments upon the stones for Moses, is being referred to in the book of Hebrews:

> For ye are not come unto the mount that might be touched, and that burned with fire, nor unto blackness, and darkness, and tempest,
> And the sound of a trumpet, and the voice of words; which voice they that heard intreated that the word should not be spoken to them any more:
> (For they could not endure that which was commanded, And if so much as a beast touch the mountain, it shall be stoned, or thrust through with a dart:
> And so terrible was the sight, that Moses said, I exceedingly fear and quake:) (Heb. 12:18-21).

The Scripture in Hebrews continues by expressly describing the countless angelic host at the heavenly Mount Sion of God:

> But ye are come unto mount Sion, and unto the city of the living God, the heavenly Jerusalem, and to an innumerable company of angels,
> To the general assembly and church of the firstborn, which are written in heaven, and to God the Judge of all, and to the spirits of just men made perfect,
> And to Jesus the mediator of the new covenant, and to the blood of sprinkling, that speaketh better things than that of Abel (Heb. 12:22-24).

The above passage from Hebrews began at God's Mount Sinai on earth with only Moses allowed to ascend it; the passage progressed by describing Moses' great fear and trembling and concludes at God's home in heaven, Mount Sion. Importantly, where earlier only Moses was allowed on God's Holy Mount, in the heavenly Jerusalem those made perfect through Jesus the mediator of the new covenant are allowed to 'come unto Mount Sion', upon the home grounds of God, and 'unto the city of the living God'. The entire 'church of the firstborn [Jesus]' will be in 'heavenly Jerusalem' called 'the city of the living God'. More importantly, under the new covenant of Jesus' shed blood sacrifice, Jesus the mediator assures the welcome entrance into the very home of God described as coming 'unto Mount Sion'. The above passage from Hebrews concludes with Christ's church consisting of each person whose name is found written in the Book of Life: 'the spirits of just men made perfect' [the saints of God before God's Incarnation made perfect by Jesus' blood on the cross], and 'an innumerable company of angels' being all welcomed and permitted to come unto God's heavenly mount.

While comparing Moses' visit to God's Mount Sinai just before the commandments were given to 'the city of the living God' at 'Mount Sion' in heaven a warning is proclaimed by God that if any being even touches God's mountain 'it shall be stoned, or thrust through with a dart' (Heb. 12:20-22). The protectors of God's Holy Mount are His specially appointed angels which are part of the 'innumerable company of angels' described in Hebrews 12:22 and the ten thousands of angels who came down on Mount Sinai to proclaim the presence of the Holy God as described in Deuteronomy 33:1-2.

We find at an earlier time God resided here on earth with only Moses permitted upon Mount Sinai. We presently have the hope of joining God as He resides in heaven where believers are part of the 'general assembly and church of the firstborn' at 'mount Sion' in 'the city of the living God, the heavenly Jerusalem'. Finally, the believing saints have assurance of finally residing again on earth in the new holy city Jerusalem where we are promised 'the tabernacle of God is with men, and he will dwell with them, and they shall be his people, and God himself shall be with them, and be their God' (Rev. 21:1-3).

The tabernacle of God is with men and He will dwell with them
On two occasions Scripture pictures thousands of angels in the presence of Jesus: first when He returns 'from heaven with his mighty angels' (2 Thess. 1:7), and again upon His return at the final Battle of

Armageddon at the valley of Megiddo 'the armies which were in heaven ... followed him upon white horses, clothed in fine linen, white and clean' (Rev. 19:11-16). Not all of our Lord's 'armies' will be made up of angels; the saints also will be an important part of Christ's armies for the Battle of Armageddon. Enoch 'prophesied of these saying, Behold, the Lord cometh with ten thousands of his saints, To execute judgment upon all, and to convince all that are ungodly among them of all their ungodly deeds which they have ungodly committed, and of all their hard speeches which ungodly sinners have spoken against him' (Jude 14-15).

As believers in Jesus we also have the hope God will again reside on earth in the New Jerusalem as viewed and heard by the eyes and ears of St. John:

> And I saw a new heaven and a new earth: for the first heaven and the first earth were passed away; and there was no more sea.
>
> And I John saw the holy city, new Jerusalem, coming down from God out of heaven, prepared as a bride adorned for her husband.
>
> And I heard a great voice out of heaven saying, Behold, the tabernacle of God is with men, and he will dwell with them, and they shall be his people, and God himself shall be with them, and be their God.
>
> And God shall wipe away all tears from their eyes; and there shall be no more death, neither sorrow, nor crying, neither shall there be any more pain: for the former things are passed away.
>
> And he that sat upon the throne said, Behold, I make all things new. And he said unto me, Write: for these words are true and faithful.
>
> And he said unto me, It is done. I am Alpha and Omega, the beginning and the end. I will give unto him that is athirst of the fountain of the water of life freely (Rev. 21:1-6).

When no more tears are shed and all who thirst are quenched with God's living water, the great voice that will be heard emanating from the New Jerusalem will be the cry heard coming from mouths of millions of angels and billions of saints crying out 'Worthy is the Lamb', never to be silenced to the ends of time.

Vast numbers of angels can be called upon by our Saviour

The number of spirits who followed Satan in his rebellion was a large number. For example, at Gadara the Lord Jesus confronted the man possessed by the powers of Satan. The evil forces inside the man identified themselves as 'Legion: for we are many' (Mark 5:9). At this time period a legion of the emperor's Roman army numbered 6,100 foot soldiers and 726 horsemen. God is all powerful and the power of Satan is limited by God.

Jesus gives us some idea of the help available to Him when He told Peter to stop his violent defence against the soldiers who arrived with Judas Iscariot to confront Jesus and take Him from the Garden of Gethsemane for His trial and crucifixion. The Lord Jesus declared to Peter that He could pray to the Father who would immediately give Him more than twelve legions of angels. This is more than 72,000 angels (Matt. 26:53). In fact, if Jesus had asked His Father He could, with just a single word, call into being countless multitudes of yet uncreated hosts of angelic beings (cf. Matt. 3:9). It is difficult to even imagine the power of over 72,000 angels when one angel had the power to kill 185,000 Assyrian soldiers in just one night (2 Kgs. 19:35)! Thankfully, Jesus came to fulfil His Father's will for our salvation.

Chapter 5

Ministering Angels to the Saints of God

The presence of holy angels should give us great comfort knowing the angels look intently into God's work of saving His people. 'Unto whom it was revealed, that not unto themselves, but unto us they did minister the things, which are now reported unto you by them that have preached the gospel unto you with the Holy Ghost sent down from heaven; *which things the angels desire to look into*' (1 Pet. 1:12). The angels' desire to look into the Gospel preaching is not just some passing interest for them. Instead, 1 Peter 1:12 conveys the same deep desire and intensity as Mary, John, and Peter had when each of them was 'looking into' the tomb of Christ after His resurrection when they each anxiously searched for Jesus' missing body (John 20:5, 11). The angels are extremely curious, desirous to understand, and eagerly observing Gospel preaching to every person.

Angels' deep desire and intensity to understand the Gospel message surely highlights the ransom price Jesus paid by His own death for the penalty incurred by humanity's sin. Scripture says, 'For he hath made him to be sin for us, who knew no sin; that we might be made the righteousness of God in him' (2 Cor. 5:21). Jesus our Lord took unto Himself the wound of separation, the very enmity and wrath of God the Father against sin. The angels probably seek to understand why the Son of God would have been willing to come in human form to prove His perfect obedience, to prove His perfect love, to show His power to live and die while staying completely attuned to His Father's will. Jesus truly lived up to God's perfection by His willing death and separation from the Father on whom He had always depended. If angels understand the true extent of the price Jesus paid on the cross, this may explain why the holy angels look intently into the Gospel message, and may explain why they seek to help man at every opportunity to come to a re-birth in the Spirit of God (See Hebrews 1:14).

Angels give encouragement in times of danger. Paul was told by an angel not to be concerned when a storm was overcoming the ship on which he was travelling to Rome:

> And now I exhort you to be of good cheer: for there shall be no loss of any man's life among you, but of the ship.
> *For there stood by me this night the angel of God*, whose I am, and whom I serve,
> Saying, Fear not, Paul; thou must be brought before Caesar: and, lo, God hath given thee all them that sail with thee.
> Wherefore, sires, be of good cheer: for I believe in God, that it shall be even as it was told me (Acts 27:22-25).

The 'angel of God' Paul spoke to on the ship may have been Jesus Himself since Paul identifies *'the angel of God, **whose I am, and whom I serve'** (Acts 27:23). If Paul states he belongs to this angel and he serves this angel, the reasonable conclusion is the angel was the visible Christ.

We who set our love upon God and God's plan of redemption are promised to be delivered by God. Therefore, we are to call upon God who promises 'and I will answer him: I will be with him in trouble; I will deliver him, and honour him' (Ps. 91:14-15). We can trust that God knows our thoughts: 'No word ever reaches my tongue, but, lo, O Lord, thou knowest it altogether' (Ps. 139:4).

God's holy angels will protect us in our time of need. When we say in our hearts daily the Lord 'is my refuge and my fortress: my God; in him will I trust' (Ps. 91:2) we are promised in Scripture:

> Because thou hast made the Lord, which is my refuge, even the most High, thy habitation;
> There shall no evil befall thee, neither shall any plague come nigh thy dwelling.
> For he shall give his angels charge over thee, to keep thee in all thy ways.
> They shall bear thee up in their hands, lest thou dash thy foot against a stone.

Thou shalt tread upon the lion and adder [cobra]: the young
lion and the dragon [Satan] shalt thou trample under feet (Ps.
91:9-13).

We can trust the power of angels. Even one of God's holy angels
has tremendous power. An example of this power is the prayerful
response of just one angel who in one night destroyed 185,000
Assyrian soldiers on behalf of God's chosen people (2 Kgs 19:35).
So awesome is the appearance of an angel some men have involuntarily
prostrated themselves before this great vision (Dan. 10:9). We may
find solace in times of trouble because Scripture teaches: *'There hath
no temptation taken you but such as is common to man: but God is faithful, who
will not suffer you to be tempted above that ye are able; but will with the temptation
also make a way to escape, that ye may be able to bear it'* (1 Cor. 10:13). Pray
for an angel to help make a way to escape in times of your greatest
temptation.

God's healing angels encamp round about making us whole
An infirm man was laying by the pool of Bethesda (translated from
Hebrew 'five porches') (John 5:2). A 'great multitude of impotent
folk, of blind, halt, withered' were 'waiting for the moving of the
water'. Scripture teaches that the Bethesda waters were then capable
of healing anyone who was first to enter the water after an angel
stirred it. 'For an angel went down at a certain season into the pool,
and troubled the water: whosoever then first after the troubling of
the water stepped in was made whole of whatsoever disease he had'
(John 5:4). Jesus chose this man to heal without an angel stirring
waters in order to glorify God (John 5:6-7).

'And a certain man was there [by the pool], which had an infirmity
thirty and eight years. When Jesus saw him lie, and knew that he had
been now a long time in that case, he saith unto him, "Wilt thou be
made whole?" The impotent man answered him, "Sir, I have no
man, when the water is troubled, to put me into the pool: but while I
am coming another steppeth down before me." Jesus saith unto
him, "Rise, take up thy bed, and walk." And immediately the man
was made whole, and took up his bed, and walked: and on the same
day was the sabbath' (John 5:5-9).

When we call upon Jesus in faith we shall be delivered unto wholeness from everything causing us fear and pain:

> I sought the Lord, and he heard me, and delivered me from all my fears. They looked unto him, and were lightened: and their faces were not ashamed. This poor man cried, and the Lord heard him, and saved him out of all his troubles.
>
> The angel of the Lord encampeth round about them that fear him, and delivereth them. O taste and see that the Lord is good: blessed is the man that trusteth in him.
>
> O fear the Lord, ye his saints: for there is no want to them that fear him. ...Many are the afflictions of the righteous: but the Lord delivereth him out of them all (Ps. 34:4-9, 19).

I urge you to join me, as I 'will bless the Lord at all times: his praise shall continually be in my mouth' (Ps. 34:1). How can we not be inspired when we know that: (1) if we look to God He will lighten us giving us the faith to never be ashamed of Him; (2) if we pray to Him God will hear us and will save us out of all our troubles; (3) if we fear and respect Him His angels will deliver us; (4) if we trust Him He will bless us; (5) if we fear and honour Him God's angels will encamp around us, providing us His provision so we shall not want; and, (6) if we seek His righteousness the Lord shall deliver us out of all our many afflictions. These are God's many inspirational promises found in Psalm 34, including the healing of our minds, souls and spirits, thus making us whole.

Peter's first prison break

Peter might not have been too surprised when the angel delivered him from prison as fully described in Acts 5:12-42. Jesus promised Peter he would live to an old age when 'another' would strengthen him 'and carry [him] whither [he] wouldest not [go]' (John 21:18). Peter was with the other apostles when they were arrested by the Sadducees. The Sadducees believed there was 'no resurrection, neither angel, nor spirit' (Acts 23:8). They were upset with the preaching of the risen Christ Jesus and especially with the many signs and wonders wrought among the people by the hands of the apostles. They were also angry about the healing power of Peter's shadow, as he walked past, crossing over the physically sick and those who were 'vexed with unclean spirits'.

The Sadducees were extremely upset because the apostles had refused to honour these religious leaders' command not to teach the risen Christ. As Peter walked along the streets he walked past the sick and demon possessed who had lined the streets because they had heard Peter's shadow, if it crossed over them, had complete healing power. Scripture explains that because of these 'many signs and wonders' among the people, multitudes of men and women were added as believers to the Lord (Acts 5:12-16).

After being arrested Peter and the apostles were put in 'the common prison'. They were released and commanded by the angel of the Lord. Scripture describes the events: *But the angel of the Lord by the night opened the prison doors, and brought them forth, and said, Go, stand and speak in the temple to the people all the words of this life'* (Acts 5:19-20). The apostles complied with the angel's direction to preach in the temple, and they departed when requested to go and speak with the council and high priest of the Sadducees (Acts 5:21, 26-27). The high priest and council asked the apostles if they did not understand the command not to teach in the name of Jesus. Importantly, when the council heard Peter's and the other apostles' answer 'they were cut to the heart, and took counsel to slay them' (Acts 5:28, 33):

> *We ought to obey God rather than men.*
> *The God of our fathers raised up Jesus, whom ye slew and hanged on a tree.*
>
> Him hath God exalted with his right hand to be a Prince and a Saviour, for to give repentance to Israel, and forgiveness of sins.
>
> And we are his witnesses of these things; and so is also the Holy Ghost, whom God hath given to them that obey him (Acts 5:29-32).

After hearing this witness by the disciples, the Sadducees council discussed killing them. A Pharisee and doctor of the law named Gamaliel (v.34) warned the council they should: 'Refrain from these men, and let them alone: for if this counsel or this work be of men, it will come to nought: But if it be of God, ye cannot overthrow it;

lest haply ye be found even to fight against God' (Acts 5:38-39). Although Scripture states the Sadducees agreed with Gamaliel, they still beat the apostles, and 'they commanded that they should not speak in the name of Jesus' before letting them go (Acts 5:40). After enduring the undeserved dishonour of imprisonment and pain of assault, the apostles went their way 'rejoicing that they were counted worthy to suffer shame for his [Jesus'] name. And daily in the temple, and in every house, they ceased not to teach and preach Jesus Christ' (Acts 5:41-42).

Peter's second prison break

Peter's second dramatic release from a prison while he was awaiting execution is another example of angels physically protecting God's saints. Peter's protection started when Herod sought the death of certain church members, including James, brother of John; Herod had killed James by the sword. (Acts 12:1-2). Peter was arrested and in prison with two Roman guards chained to him. Two other guards were standing watch on the night before Peter was to be brought before Herod:

> And, behold, the angel of the Lord came upon him, and a light shined in the prison: and he smote Peter on the side, and raised him up, saying, Arise up quickly. And his chains fell off from his hands.
>
> And the angel said unto him, Gird thyself, and bind on thy sandals. And so he did. And he saith unto him, Cast thy garment about thee, and follow me.
>
> And he went out, and followed him; and wist not that it was true which was done by the angel; but thought he saw a vision.
>
> When they were past the first and second ward, they came unto the iron gate that leadeth unto the city; which opened to them of his [the angel's] own accord: and they went out, and passed on through one street; and forthwith the angel departed from him.
>
> And when Peter was come to himself, he said, Now I know of surety, that the Lord hath sent his angel, and hath delivered me out of the hand of Herod, and from all the expectation of the people of the Jews (Acts 12:7-11).

Angels come by God's everlasting, immutable mercy and love
The manifold mercies of God are demonstrated by His angels 'sent
out to render service for the sake of those who will inherit salvation'
(Heb. 1:14; cf. 12:22). In the Holy Scripture God informs us of His
wonderful nature of forgiveness as promised in his covenant of love:
'And shewing mercy unto thousands of them that love me, and keep
my commandments' (Exod. 20:6). The Hebrew word for mercy is
'*hesed*' which is God's steadfast covenant love. 'Every good gift and
every perfect gift is from above, and cometh down from the Father
of lights, with whom is no variableness, neither shadow of turning.
Of his own will begat he us with the word of truth, that we should
be a kind of firstfruits of his creatures' (Jas 1:17-18).

God's love and mercy for mankind is perfectly consistent and never
ending (Ps. 100:5 'his mercy is everlasting'; see Psalm 117:2; 118:1).
His character is immutable, never changing (Mal. 3:6 'I am the Lord,
I change not'). 'The immutability of his counsel, [He] confirmed it
by an oath: ... it was impossible for God to lie' (Heb. 6:17-18). His
perfection, holiness, love, truthfulness, goodness and faithfulness
remain the same from the beginning to the end because God has no
beginning and no end. 'Art thou not from everlasting, O Lord my
God, mine Holy One?' (Hab. 1:12).

God cannot lie or distort the truth; in fact Jesus says of God 'thy
word is truth' (John 17:17). 'The word of the Lord is right; and all his
works are done in truth... The counsel of the Lord standeth for ever,
the thoughts of his heart to all generations' (Ps. 33:4, 11).

God will not accept evil by anyone, be it man or angel, because
He cannot do evil (Ps. 5:4-5 'For thou art not a God that hath pleasure
in wickedness: neither shall evil dwell with thee. The foolish shall
not stand in thy sight: thou hatest all workers of iniquity' see also Job
34:10). 'Thou art of purer eyes than to behold evil, and canst not
look on iniquity' (Hab. 1:13). Jesus was quite specific when He warns
that at the time of judgment He will say to those not written in the
Lamb's Book of Life: 'I never knew you: depart from me, ye that
work iniquity' (Matt. 7:23).

'Wherefore now let the fear of the Lord be upon you; take heed
and do it: for there is no iniquity with the Lord our God, nor respect
of persons' (2 Chron. 19:7). God will never overlook evil. We are

warned to 'remember the days of darkness; for they shall be many. All that cometh is vanity. Rejoice, O young man, in thy youth; and let thy heart cheer thee in the days of thy youth, and walk in the ways of thine heart, and in the sight of thine eyes: but know thou, that for all these things God will bring thee into judgment' (Eccles. 11:8, 9). 'God shall judge the righteous and the wicked: for there is a time for every purpose and for every work' (Eccles. 3:17). God cannot consider evil and will never solicit us to do evil: 'for God cannot be tempted with evil, neither tempteth he any man' (Jas. 1:13).

We can trust Scripture because, as Balaam spoke the Word of the Lord: 'God is not a man, that he should lie' (Num. 23:19). God is beyond our shortsighted ignorance, lack of love, foolish immaturity and other inconsistent qualities which we use to try understand God's steadfast covenant love for all who have accepted His Son as Lord. 'For this is my [God's] covenant unto them, when I shall take away their sins' (Rom. 11:29). God's glory is incorruptible (Rom. 1:23). We truly can have 'hope of eternal life, which God, that cannot lie, promised before the world began' (Titus 1:2).

Angels are spirits sent by God to accomplish His will among human beings by ministering and by bringing messages of good news. Angels also bring God's power upon the unbelieving so as to influence doubting men by the righteous power of the Lord. (See Daniel 4:28-37). Even though men's hearts may beat fast with fear upon the sight of angels of the Lord, the angels seek to comfort us with the words, 'Fear not' (Luke 1:13). The Lord promises that 'them that feared the Lord, and that thought upon his name ... shall be mine ... in that day when I make up my jewels; and I will spare them, as a man spareth his own son that serveth him' (Mal. 3:16-17).

In the presence of angels some will not taste death

'The chariots of God' in Psalm 68:17 are revealed to be 'twenty thousand, even thousands of angels'. The chariots of God appear for various purposes, including war, protection of the saints and glory for God through the visible translation of His prophet Elijah (2 Kgs. 2:3). Only one other has not tasted death: 'And Enoch walked with God: and he was not; for God took him' (Gen. 5:24); 'By faith Enoch was translated that he should not see death' (Heb. 11:5).

Before Christ's return to Mount Megiddo we are told to comfort one another with the words that describe the living saints on earth as also being translated without facing death: 'we which are alive and remain shall be caught up together with them in the clouds, to meet the Lord in the air: and so shall we ever be with the Lord' (1 Thess. 4:17). Just before we are 'caught up' with Christ, Jesus will be announced by an archangel: 'For the Lord himself shall descend from heaven with a shout, with the voice of the archangel, and with the trump of God: and the dead in Christ shall rise first' (1 Thess. 4:16).

The angel of the Lord and Spirit may work together for salvation
Philip was able to preach Jesus to the Ethiopian eunuch who was travelling by chariot. The eunuch was moved to cry out: 'I believe that Jesus Christ is the Son of God' as he was led to salvation and was baptized in the Spirit (Acts 8:35-38; see Galatians 3:26-27). Philip did not just happen across the Ethiopian, rather 'the angel of the Lord spake unto Philip, saying, Arise and go toward the south unto the way that goeth down from Jerusalem unto Gaza, which is desert' (Acts 8:26). When Philip came upon the Ethiopian who was reading Scripture and in his heart seeking understanding, 'the Spirit said unto Philip, Go near, and join thyself to this chariot' (Acts 8:28-34).

After completing his preaching, 'the Spirit of the Lord caught away Philip, that the eunuch saw him no more: and he went on his way rejoicing. But Philip was found at Azotus: and passing through he preached in all the cities, till he came to Caesarea' (Acts 8:39-40).

The angel, the Gentile centurion and Peter
St. Peter first brought the Gospel to the Gentiles with the direction, vision and guidance of an angel of God and the Spirit of God (Acts 10-11). This miraculous story begins:

> There was a certain man in Caesarea called Cornelius, a centurion of the band called the Italian band, A devout man, and one that feared God with all his house, which gave much alms to the people, and prayed to God alway[s].
> He saw in a vision evidently about the ninth hour of the day an angel of God coming in to him, and saying unto him, Cornelius. And when he looked on him, he was afraid, and said, What is it,

Lord? And he said unto him, Thy prayers and thine alms are come up for a memorial before God.

And now send men to Joppa, and call for one Simon, whose surname is Peter: He lodgeth with one Simon a tanner, whose house is by the sea side: he shall tell thee what thou oughtest to do.

And when the angel which spake unto Cornelius was departed, he called two of his household servants, and a devout soldier of them that waited on him continually; And when he had declared all these things unto them, he sent them to Joppa (Acts 10:1-8).

The story is best explained by Peter himself as he justifies his action of bringing the Gospel to the Gentiles. Peter, when challenged, explained the conversion of Cornelius to the apostles and brethren. They heard that Peter brought the Word of God to the Gentiles, who were called the 'uncircumcised', and that Peter actually had eaten with them:

I was in the city of Joppa praying: and in a trance I saw a vision, a certain vessel descend, as it had been a great sheet, let down from heaven by four corners; and it came even to me: Upon the which when I had fastened mine eyes, I considered, and saw fourfooted beasts of the earth, and wild beasts, and creeping things, and fowls of the air.

And I heard a voice saying unto me, Arise, Peter; slay and eat.

But I said, Not so, Lord: for nothing common or unclean hath at any time entered into my mouth.

But the voice answered me again from heaven, What God hath cleansed, that call not thou common. And this was done three times: and all were drawn up again into heaven.

And, behold, immediately there were three men already come unto the house where I was, sent from Caesarea unto me. And *the Spirit bade me go with them*, nothing doubting. Moreover these six brethren accompanied me, and we entered into the man's house:

And he shewed us *how he had seen an angel in his house*, which stood and said unto him, Send men to Joppa, and call for Simon, whose surname is Peter; Who shall tell thee words, whereby thou and all thy house shall be saved.

And as I began to speak, the Holy Ghost fell on them, as on us at the beginning.

Then I remembered the word of the Lord [Jesus], how that he said, *John indeed baptized with water; but ye shall be baptized with the Holy Ghost.*

Forasmuch then as God gave them the like gift as he did unto us, who believed on the Lord Jesus Christ, what was I, that I could withstand God?

When they heard these things, they [the apostles and brethren] held their peace, and glorified God, saying, Then hath God also to the Gentiles granted repentance unto life (Acts 11:5-18).

God has joy in each of His children when they turn from the world by accepting His sacrificial Son and thus becoming His adopted children (Gal. 3:26-29). The host of heaven share God's happiness: 'There is joy in the presence of the angels of God over one sinner who repents' (Luke 15:10). Your prayers are heard and if it is the will of God, He will send His angel to show you His favour, as Cornelius was shown favour (Acts 10:1-8; 11:1-18).

We may not see the angels as they minister to our spiritual and physical needs; pray for God's strength and He will send His angel or angels so we can do God's work. At a time of great tribulation and utter frustration, Elijah, one of the greatest men of faith in God, was provided food and water by 'the angel of the Lord'. The angel of the Lord encouraged Elijah twice to eat for the necessary strength to travel forty days and nights unto Horeb the mount of God (1 Kgs. 19:5-8).

He therefore that ministereth to you the Spirit, and worketh miracles among you, doeth he it by the works of the law, or by the hearing of faith?

Wherefore then serveth the law? It was added because of transgressions, *till the seed should come to whom the promise was made; and it was ordained by angels in the hand of a mediator. Now a mediator is not a mediator of one, but God is one.*

Is the law then against the promises of God? God forbid: for if there had been a law given which could have given life, verily righteousness should have been by the law.

But the scripture hath concluded all under sin, that the promise by faith of Jesus Christ might be given to them that believe (Gal. 3:5,19-22).

The Jewish scholars called the angel of the Lord by the name *'Metatron, the angel of countenance'*, because He witnesses the countenance of God continuously and works to fulfil the design of God for each of us, just as the angel of the Lord encouraged and worked to help Elijah carry forth his calling for God. In the Old Testament 'the angel of the Lord' may have frequently been the Incarnate Jesus. Whereas, 'the angel of God' referred to in the New Testament very well may be the pre-Incarnate Jesus when appearing after His death and ascension into heaven, as mentioned when Paul, on the ship, spoke to and identified 'the angel of God, whose I am, and whom I serve' (Acts 27:23).

The angelic face of Stephen

When Stephen, the first martyr for Jesus, died he cried out calling upon God saying, 'Lord Jesus receive my spirit' (Acts 7:59). Importantly, Stephen understood the commandments of Jesus to love God and your neighbour. He asked for the Lord to forgive the sin of those who were killing him, even while the stones were yet striking him (Acts 7:59-60). The story of Stephen's 'trial' by the high priest begins with the council looking steadfastly on him, seeing 'his face as it had been the face of an angel' (Acts 6:15).

Stephen's sermon to the council included references to angels. While discussing Moses' call to serve he said: 'And when forty years were expired in the wilderness of mount Sinai an angel of the Lord in a flame of fire in a bush' appeared to him and 'the voice of the Lord came unto him, Saying, I am the God of thy fathers...' (Acts 7:30-31; also Exod. 3:2). Stephen continued his sermon by describing God's reaction to how the people turned away from God during their wilderness travel when the people: 'said unto Aaron, Make us gods to go before us, ... they made a calf, ... offered sacrifice unto the idol, and rejoiced in the works of their own hands. *Then God turned, and gave them up to worship the host of heaven ...* '(Acts 7:40-42). The host of heaven God refers to appears to be 'his angels he charged with folly' in Job 4:18.

The conviction of the high priest and his council was great as Stephen again spoke of the nature of angels and wilfulness of these men against the Holy Spirit:

Ye stiffnecked and uncircumcised in heart and ears, ye do always resist the Holy Ghost: as your fathers did, so do ye.

Which of the prophets have not your fathers persecuted? and they have slain them which shewed before of the coming of the Just One; of whom ye have been now the betrayers and murderers:

Who have received the law by the disposition of angels, and have not kept it (Acts 7:51-53).

Just before his death Stephen, 'being full of the Holy Ghost, looked up stedfastly into heaven, and saw the glory of God, and Jesus standing on the right hand of God' (Acts 7:55). Here, we see a picture of Jesus as He stands before His Father to receive Stephen. Jesus might honour those who have been and are presently being martyred for His name by standing to meet them, but Scripture does not make this clear. The Book of Revelation makes clear that all saints martyred in the Tribulation period will be clothed in white linen praising God at the throne and having all their tears wiped from their eyes by the Lamb (Rev. 7:9-17).

Trust in the Word of God and pray for help from God's angels
We are told to trust by hearing the Word and not by sight. (2 Cor. 5:7). This command includes God's Word about angels. Those who deny the heavenly holy host because angels have not been seen are men who make excuses for their lack of faith. We all trust in things unseen every day like planes flying on unseen air or lights illuminating by unseen electricity. Everything we see is made up of unseen matter at the microscopic level. 'While we look not at the things which are seen, but at the things which are not seen: for the things which are seen are temporal; but the things which are not seen are eternal' (2 Cor. 4:18).

Trust God for He does not lie when we are lovingly told: 'For he shall give his angels charge over thee, to keep thee in all thy ways. They shall bear thee up in their hands, lest thou dash thy foot against a stone' (Ps. 91:11-12). Pray for God's help by His angels or through the Holy Spirit who indwells those who place their trust in our Lord Jesus; 'If God be for us who can be against us? He that spared not his own Son, but delivered him up for us all, how shall he not with him also freely give us all things?' (Rom. 8:31-32). 'And this is the confidence that we have in him, that, if we ask any thing according to his will, he heareth us: and if we know that he hear us, whatsoever we ask, we know that we have the petitions that we desired of him' (1 John 5:14-15).

As a child many of us were blessed by family members who read Bible stories to us. Stories were told to us about the den of lions and an overheated furnace where God intervened to protect His own by sending His angel. Daniel, the prophet of God, had the privilege of not only being protected by God's angel but the privilege of seeing the angel: 'My God hath sent his angel, and hath shut the lions' mouths' (Dan. 6:22). You might recall how Daniel, because of his open prayer to Jehovah in violation to the king's decree, was locked in overnight with three hungry lions. But in the morning Daniel was not harmed 'because [Daniel] believed in his God' (Dan. 6:12-23).

Will any of us who have heard the story of Shadrach, Meshach and Abed-nego, ever forget the Hebrew children who refused to worship the king of Babylon and were cast bound into the roaring furnace of fire and smoke. And, how God sent His angel to protect them in a furnace so hot it killed the men who came close enough to throw the boys in. The boys were not hurt, nor was their hair singed, and they had no smell of the flaming smoke which had surrounded them. King Nebuchadnezzar could see the boys walking around with a fourth person in the furnace of raging fire whom the king described as: 'like the Son of God' (Dan. 3:20-27).

Daniel and the Hebrew boys were shown great favour in the pagan society because the king was so impressed with the supernatural angelic protection shown them as believers and followers of 'the living God' and 'the Most High God'.

Chapter 6

Three Heavens? Home of God and His angels?

Some questions are raised with the various scriptural descriptions of heaven, apparently describing 'heaven' as being more than one place!

The first heaven
Physically we now know there is a clear demarcation between a 'heaven' – the first heaven – consisting of earth's atmosphere and a 'heaven' consisting of outer space – the second heaven. In the most recent past through the far-searching Hubble telescope we now know there appears to be a physical end to the ever expanding space, with Scripture describing a 'heaven' beyond – the third heaven.

The first heaven is described as 'the heaven stayed from dew' in Haggai 1:10 and the effect of Elijah's prayer resulting in the heaven giving rain, and the earth bringing forth her fruit (Jas 5:18). (Elijah's prayers are inferred from 1 Kings 17:1 and 18:42.)

The first heaven of earth's atmosphere reaches above the earth's surface to the boundary with outer space. Earth's atmosphere consists of layers commonly known as the atmosphere, troposphere, stratosphere, mesosphere, ionosphere and the exosphere.

The Pharisees demanded a 'sign from heaven' in their endeavour to tempt Jesus to prove He was the Messiah. If Jesus had wanted to provide such a 'sign from heaven' He probably would have displayed it as a celestial portent visible above earth. He declined such a temptation, yet we should know His power was sufficient for any such sign He requested. But, of course, any such sign would have originated from His Father above in the third heaven since Jesus made abundantly clear His acts were of His Father and to glorify the Father's name. Consider Jesus' prayer in the Garden of Gethsemane: 'Abba, Father, all things are possible unto thee; take away this cup from me: nevertheless not what I will, but what thou wilt' (Mark 14:36).

The second heaven

Clearly, other heavens beyond the atmospheric skies of earth are spoken of in Scripture. A second heaven reaches out past earth's atmosphere to the ends of outer space. Using the Hubble telescope, the furthest galaxy was recently discovered at the near edge of the far corner of space. This galaxy is located about thirteen billion light years away from earth. Since a light year equals six trillion miles this newly discovered galaxy is approximately thirteen billion times six trillion miles away!

The end of the cosmos, outer space, describes the boundary of the second heaven. Psalm 19:1 speaks about the second heaven of outer space above the earth's atmosphere containing the sun and stars and other wonders of the sky: 'The heavens declare the glory of God; and the firmament sheweth his handiwork.'

The difference between the first and second heavens in Scripture is blurred at times:

> And there shall be signs in the sun, and in the moon, and in the stars; and upon the earth distress of nations, with perplexity; the sea and the waves roaring;
> Men's hearts failing them for fear, and for looking after those things which are coming on the earth: for the powers of heaven shall be shaken.
> And then shall they see the Son of man coming in a cloud with power and great glory.
> And when these things begin to come to pass, then look up, and lift up your heads; for your redemption draweth nigh (Luke 21:25-28).

The third heaven

Scripture tells us that God's throne is in heaven (Is. 66:1; Acts 7:49). And, God looks down from heaven for those men who 'understand and seek God' (Ps. 14:2; 53:2).

Is the heaven high above the earth described in Psalm 103:11 the same location of God's throne and the heaven described as the heaven above which cannot be measured in Jeremiah 31:37? Heaven high above earth which cannot be measured surely is not the heaven of our earthly atmosphere or the depths of outer space, but it is instead the place where all who have died in faith 'desire a better country, that is, an heavenly: wherefore God is not ashamed to be called their God: for he hath prepared for them a city' (Heb. 11:16).

The third heaven of God's throne is spoken of as the returning place of the angel in Luke 2:8-15 where 'the angel of the Lord' accompanied by 'a multitude of heavenly host praising God' brought good tidings of our Savour's birth to the shepherds. The heavenly host and the angel of the Lord then returned 'away from them into heaven'.

In response to Nathanael's exclamation that Jesus was the Messianic Deity, 'the Son of God', and was the Jewish political messianic hope, 'the King of Israel', Jesus describes one of the 'greater things' Nathanael would see of Him to prove He is the Son of God and King of Israel (John 1:47-49). Jesus' description of this proof, what will yet come upon His ascension into heaven, has been named one of Jesus' 'seven great signs':

Verily, verily, I say unto you, Hereafter ye shall see heaven open, and the angels of God ascending and descending upon the Son of man (John 1:51).

'Heaven open' is a symbol of the fellowship available with the Father to believers in Christ; the power of the mediating sacrifice of the blood of the cross opens heaven for fellowship. In Jesus' description above, the angels of God must be coming from the heavenly home of God in the third heaven since the angels are ascending and descending from the opened heaven. Jacob also describes his vision of watching angels coming and going from heaven's gate (Gen. 28:12).

Again, referring to the home of God, a great wonder in heaven occurs when the Lamb 'had opened the seventh seal, there was silence in heaven about the space of half an hour' (Rev. 8:1). The most frequent referral to the heavenly home of God is Luke 11:2: 'And he said unto them, "When ye pray, say, *Our Father which art in heaven*, Hallowed be thy name. Thy kingdom come, Thy will be done, as in heaven, so in earth."'

St. Paul speaks of being 'caught up to the third heaven' and that 'he was caught up into paradise, and heard unspeakable words, which it is not lawful for a man to utter' (2 Cor. 12:1-4). We will learn the mystery of God's dwelling place in the third heaven of paradise when we, as saints in Christ Jesus, are 'caught up' with Him as described in the rapture of believers in 1 Thessalonians 4:16-17: 'the Lord himself shall descend from heaven with a shout, with the voice of the archangel, and with the trump of God: and the dead in Christ shall rise first: Then we which are alive and remain shall be caught up together with them in the clouds, to meet the Lord in the air: and so shall we ever be with the Lord.'

Jesus' saints who are 'caught up together with them in the clouds' will start their journey in 'the clouds' of the first heaven in earth's atmosphere. The promise of 'ever being with the Lord', may begin in the first heaven of earth's atmosphere, at least for a brief period of time. Our 'ever being with the Lord' refers more specifically to our sojourn in the third heaven, until returning to earth to reign over the earth as the saints of Jesus during the thousand year Millennium. (Rev. 20:6). 'Behold he cometh with clouds; and every eye shall see him' (Rev. 1:7). Always be watching and waiting for His return because the exact 'day and that hour knoweth no man, no, not the angels which are in heaven, neither the Son, but the Father' (Mark 13:32.)

In the first heaven, Jesus was carried up as the disciples watched: 'he was taken up; and a cloud received him out of their sight. And while they looked stedfastly toward heaven as he went up, behold two men [angels] stood by them in white apparel; Which also said, Ye men of Galilee, why stand ye gazing up into heaven? this same Jesus, which is taken up from you into heaven, shall so come in like manner as ye have seen him go into heaven' (Acts 1:9-11).

Jesus promised that upon His return, His second coming, to earth to rule men everyone 'shall see the Son of man coming in the clouds of heaven with power and great glory' (Matt. 24:30; see also Matthew 26:64; Mark 13:26; 14:62; Luke 21:27). *For as the lightning cometh out of the east, and shineth even unto the west; so shall also the coming of the Son of man be. For wheresoever the carcase is, there will the eagles be gathered together* (Matt. 24:27-28.)

Revelation 6:16-17 describes 'the wrath of the Lamb' as 'the great day of his wrath is come' during the end times of the Great Tribulation. Whereas 1 Thessalonians 1:10 and 5:9-11 describe *the elect of the church being taken to heaven* before the Tribulation begins. 'God hath not appointed us to wrath' (1 Thess. 5:9). As we 'wait for his Son from heaven' we are assured as believers in Jesus that we are to be 'delivered from the wrath to come' (1 Thess. 1:10). Here again Scripture refers to the third heaven.

Jesus spoke of beholding 'Satan as lightning fall from heaven' in Luke 10:18 which is when the Lord God cast him out of heaven for his wilful rebellion. Satan's fall is described in Ezekiel 28:11-19: Satan was cast from the 'mountain of God' and from the 'midst of the stones of fire' at the throne of God in the third heaven.

Although he was cast down from the third heaven at the time of his first rebellion, Satan was allowed to return for the purpose of accusing the brethren of God (Job 1:6). However, there will come a time when Satan is cast out of the third heaven down to the earth. Revelation describes a war in heaven leading to Satan and his unholy angels being cast down to earth so that they were no longer found in heaven. However, before this decisive war, God suffered Satan before Him day and night allowing him to accuse the brethren:

> And there was a war in heaven: Michael and his angels fought against the dragon; and the dragon fought and his angels,
>
> And prevailed not; neither was their place found any more in heaven.
>
> And the great dragon was cast out, that old serpent, called the Devil, and Satan, which deceiveth the whole world: he was cast out into the earth, and his angels were cast out with him.
>
> And I heard a loud voice saying in heaven, Now is come salvation, and strength, and the kingdom of our God, and the power of his Christ: for the accuser of our brethren is cast down, which accused them before our God day and night.
>
> And they overcame him by the blood of the Lamb, and by the word of their testimony; and they loved not their lives unto the death.
>
> Therefore rejoice, ye heavens, and ye that dwell in them. Woe to the inhabiters of the earth and of the sea! for the devil is come

down unto you, having great wrath, because he knoweth that he hath but a short time (Rev. 12:7-12).

God's throne is in the third heaven

The third heaven is the residence of God. 'The Lord is in his holy temple, the Lord's throne is in heaven' (Ps. 11:4). And, 'the Lord hath prepared his throne in the heavens; and his kingdom ruleth over all' (Ps. 103:19). And finally, 'Thus saith the Lord, The heaven is my throne, and the earth is my footstool: where is the house that ye build unto me? and where is the place of my rest?' (Is. 66:1; compare Acts 7:49). At the right hand of God Jesus Christ resides, in the third heaven: 'So then after the Lord had spoken unto them, he was received up into heaven, and sat on the right hand of God' (Mark 16:19). 'After this I beheld, and, lo, a great multitude, which no man could number, of all nations, and kindreds, and people, and tongues, stood before the throne, and before the Lamb, clothed with white robes, and palms in their hands; And cried with a loud voice, saying, Salvation to our God which sitteth upon the throne, and unto the Lamb' (Rev. 7:9-10).

The third heaven where God resides is beyond the end of space as we know it. Some believe the third heaven is north of earth. Job 26:7 vividly describes God's handiwork: 'He stretcheth out the north over the empty place, and hangeth the earth upon nothing.' Interestingly, the Hubble space telescope has revealed what our eyes cannot see. If we look with the naked eye to the northern sky it appears as though it is as full of stars as everywhere else in the sky. On the other hand, the space telescope reveals that the north sky is empty of all stars, a cone of emptiness out to the ends of visible space! Lucifer's fall first started after seeking to ascend into heaven, exalting his throne above the holy angels of God, and seeking to 'sit also upon the mount of the congregation, in the sides of the north' (Is. 14:13).

All three heavens and the earth belong to God the Creator

Psalm 115:16-17 refers to the three spheres created by God: heaven which is God's dwelling place; earth which God gave to the children of men; and, 'silence', which is the place where the dead do not praise

God. Verse 15 leaves no doubt who created all: 'Ye are blessed of the Lord which made heaven and earth.' Man may have some possessory rights to earth and in Genesis man is told to have dominion over it, yet always everything belongs to God: 'Behold, the heaven and the heaven of heavens is the Lord's thy God, the earth also, with all that therein is' (Deut. 10:14). Here, verse 14 speaks of at least two separate heavens, with perhaps the first heaven referred to as 'the heaven', including both the earth's atmosphere and outer space to the ends of the cosmos, while 'the heaven of heavens' describes God's home and throne.

The mountain of God is the place of His presence in visible glory, whether it is in any of the heavens or upon earth. For example, when Moses took Aaron, Nadab, Abihu and the seventy chosen elders of Israel to the foot of the mount of God, Moses was allowed to continue upon the mount and come into the presence of God; Moses observed: 'There was under his feet as it were a paved work of a sapphire stone [transparent sky blue], and as it were the body of heaven in his clearness. ... And the sight of the glory of the Lord was like devouring fire on the top of the mount' (Exod. 24:10, 17). All 'is the Lord's thy God' (Deut. 10:14).

Chapter 7

Jacob's Vision of Angels at Heaven's Gate

The Need for Prayer, Worship and Trust in God's Word

Jacob's famous vision of the ladder leading from earth to heaven occurred after he had received his father Isaac's blessing. Jacob had tricked Isaac into believing that Jacob was Esau, his older bother. Jacob's vision came to him later when he was honouring his father's command to travel to the land of Padan-aram where he was to meet and live with Rebekah's brother Laban.

During Jacob's trip between Beer-sheba and Haran he stopped at a place he later named Bethel meaning 'house of God'. Jacob apparently was renaming this place because Scripture states: 'the name of that city was called Luz at the first' (Gen. 28:19). Jacob's vision occurs at night after he has lied down. He lay down in an open area using a large stone as his 'pillow' (Gen. 28:11). Jacob's vision was of God who made a covenant blessing with Jacob:

> And he dreamed, and behold a ladder set up on the earth, and the top of it reached to heaven: and behold the angels of God ascending and descending on it.
>
> And, behold, the Lord stood above it, and said, I am the Lord God of Abraham thy father, and the God of Isaac: the land whereon thou liest, to thee will I give it, and to thy seed;
>
> And thy seed shall be as the dust of the earth, and thou shalt spread abroad to the west, and to the east, and to the north, and to the south: and in thee and in thy seed shall all the families of the earth be blessed.
>
> And, behold, I am with thee, and will keep thee in all places, whither thou goest, and will bring thee again into this land; for I will not leave thee, until I have done that which I have spoken to thee of (Gen. 28:12-15).

Jacob was thankful to the Lord as we all should be when our prayers are met. After receiving his blessing Jacob built an altar to God and worshipped Him in fear. Jacob made his own promise to God pledging he would return a tithe of all he possessed to God:

> And Jacob awaked out of his sleep, and he said, Surely the Lord is in this place; and I knew it not.
>
> And he was afraid, and said, How dreadful is this place! this is none other but the house of God, and this is the gate of heaven.
>
> And Jacob rose up early in the morning, and took the stone that he had put for his pillows, and set it up for a pillar, and poured oil upon the top of it.
>
> And he called the name of that place Beth-el ...
>
> And Jacob vowed a vow, saying, If God will be with me, and will keep me in this way that I go, and will give me bread to eat, and raiment to put on,
>
> So that I come again to my father's house in peace; then shall the Lord shall be my God:
>
> And this stone, which I have set for a pillar, shall be God's house: and of all that thou shalt give me I will surely give the tenth unto thee (Gen. 28:16-22).

God's promised blessing came quickly to Jacob after he reached the land of Laban; the land of his mother Rebekah's brother. Jacob recognized in his heart the lifelong blessing he had received from the Lord when he first saw Laban's daughter Rachel. Jacob knew she was the one chosen of God for him: 'when Jacob saw Rachel ... Jacob kissed Rachel, and lifted up his voice, and wept' (Gen. 29:10, 11). Later, in answer to God's direction, Jacob again went to Bethel to build another altar (Gen. 35:1). Again, another blessing follows Jacob as he honours God's word of direction:

> So Jacob came to Luz, which is in the land of Canaan, that is, Beth-el, he and all the people that were with him.
>
> And he built there an altar, and called the place El-beth-el: because there God appeared unto him, when he fled from the face of his brother [El-beth-el means 'God of Beth-el'] (Gen. 35:6-7).

When Jacob came out of Padan-aram God appeared, blessed him and returned to heaven. We see Jacob's response and his renaming of the place:

> And God said unto him, I am God Almighty: be fruitful and multiply; a nation and a company of nations shall be of thee, and kings shall come out of thy loins;
> and the land which I gave Abraham and Isaac, to thee I will give it, and to thy seed after thee will I give the land.
> And God went up from him in the place where he talked with him.
> And Jacob set up a pillar in the place where he talked with him, even a pillar of stone: and he poured a drink offering thereon, and he poured oil thereon.
> And Jacob called the name of the place where God spake with him, Beth-el (Gen. 35:10-15).

Jacob prays for deliverance from his brother Esau

As you will recall, Jacob had tricked Esau out of his birthright causing Esau to become extremely angry with him. Many years later Jacob returned to Beer-sheba to meet his brother Esau. Seeking God's protection during the upcoming meeting Jacob had 'offered sacrifice upon the mount, and called his brethren [family] to eat bread: and they did eat bread, and tarried all night in the mount' (Gen. 31:54). Jacob was shown great favour by God in this time of fear and apprehension. Scripture describes: 'Jacob went on his way, and the angels of God met him. And when Jacob saw them, he said This is God's host: and he called the name of the place Mahanaim [meaning "double camp" referring to the angel's and Jacob's companies]' (Gen. 32:1-2). If this visual appearance of angels was not enough, Jacob had a physical encounter with 'the angel' just before he met Esau. In the book of Hosea Jacob is said to have 'had power over the angel, and prevailed: he wept, and made supplication unto him: he found him in Bethel [meaning "house of God"]' (Hos. 12:4).

Prior to this encounter with 'the angel', Jacob prays in earnest:
O God of my father Abraham, and God of my father Isaac, the Lord which saidst unto me, Return unto thy country, and to thy kindred, and I will deal well with thee:

I am not worthy of the least of all the mercies, and of all the truth, which thou hast shewed unto thy servant; for with my staff I passed over this Jordan; and now I am become two bands. [In fear of Esau's violent attack Jacob had separated his party in two groups so at least one group could survive the assault.](Gen. 32:7-8).

Deliver me, I pray thee, from the hand of my brother, from the hand of Esau: for I fear him, lest he will come and smite me, and the mother with the children.

And thou saidst, I will surely do thee good, and make thy seed as the sand of the sea, which cannot be numbered for multitude (Gen. 32:9-12).

After this earnest pray for deliverance, Jacob arose during the night and sent his two wives Rachel and Leah, and everyone else in his party across the river Jabbok;

Jacob was left alone; and there wrestled a man [the angel] with him until the breaking of the day.

And when he saw that he prevailed not against him, he touched the hollow of his thigh; and the hollow of Jacob's thigh was out of joint, as he wrestled with him.

And he said, Let me go, for the day breaketh. And he said, I will not let thee go, except thou bless me.

And he said unto him, What is thy name? And he said, Jacob.

And he said, Thy name shall be called no more Jacob, but Israel: for as a prince hast thou power with God and with men, and hast prevailed.

And Jacob asked him, and said, Tell me, I pray thee, thy name. And he said, Wherefore is it that thou dost ask after my name? And he blessed him there.

And Jacob called the name of the place Peniel: for I have seen God face to face, and my life is preserved.

And as he passed over Peniel the sun rose upon him, and he halted upon his thigh.

Therefore the children of Israel eat not of the sinew which shrank, which is upon the hollow of the thigh, unto this day: because he touched the hollow of Jacob's thigh in the sinew that shrank (Gen. 32:24-32).

Jacob departed from this encounter with a new name, Israel, which means: 'he fights or persists with God' (in prevailing prayer). The 'el' in Israel means 'god'. Jacob received the blessing from God because he refused to release his grip on the angel until he was blessed. Peniel, the place where they wrestled means 'the face of God'.

Finally, after a surprisingly peaceful meeting with Esau, Jacob travelled to a place where he purchased a parcel of land, and he erected an altar to honour God, which he named '*El-elohe-Israel*' meaning 'a Mighty God is the God of Israel'.

Do not doubt God's answer to prayers if given by an angel
God will answer the prayers of righteous men by sending His messengers, His angels (Luke 1:13). We should rejoice because in special times we may see angels. Some people will understand in their hearts these angels are sent by God. The Bible tells us an angel of the Lord was sent to John the Baptist's father, Zacharias, while he was worshipping God in the temple of the Lord. God's angel messenger, Gabriel, had come to Zacharias from standing in the presence of God. Gabriel came to give him good news concerning the birth of a son. Gabriel was pleased to do God's will by bringing to Zacharias 'these glad tidings' (Luke 1:19).

Angels minister by actions as well as words of comfort. On occasion humans have been seriously affected by the power given to angels through the judgment of God. Zacharias stands as a warning to all that the messages of God should not be challenged by doubt. When responding to the angel Gabriel's message of John's birth and John's filling by the Holy Ghost, Zacharias was doubtful because of his wife Elisabeth and his own old age. In response to this doubt the angel answered: 'I am Gabriel, that stand in the presence of God; and am sent to speak unto thee, and to show thee these glad tidings. And behold, thou shalt be dumb, and not able to speak, until the day that these things shall be performed, because thou believest not my words, which shall be fulfilled in their season' (Luke 1:18-20). Some powerful angels, like Gabriel, have the wonderful privilege and honour to stand in the presence of God. Even Moses was not allowed to see the face of God 'for there shall no man see me, and live' (Exod. 33:20).

Zacharias was overcome by fear upon the sight of the angel Gabriel. Even though troubled and with great fear, Zacharias still refused to believe. God will not be mocked by doubt when He sends His angel messengers to us for there is no power but of God and all powers that be are ordained by God (Rom. 13:1).

Zacharias, although a priest of the Lord, still had unbelief and doubted that God could do as Gabriel had told him. This was a man raised to be a priest in God's temple. As one of God's priests Zacharias would know that it is impossible for man to know the depth of the riches of the wisdom and knowledge of God. Thus, Zacharias should have trusted in the word of the Lord (Rom. 11:33). The Psalmist proclaimed 'the Lord how great are thy works!' (Ps. 92:5). Through the wrath of God Zacharias knew his muteness was a small measure. Zacharias knew the story of Job and how his glory was stripped from him and his crown taken from his head. Unlike Job, who was counted as one of God's enemies by the wrath he suffered, Zacharias was but temporarily subdued by silence (Job 19:9-11).

We should be looking, listening and praying for the Word of God because we have been commanded to hear the Word of the Lord. But we should also be praying that we will be more like Daniel than Zacharias so we will know the Lord's Word when the angels bring it to us so we might tremble at His Word for the glory of His name's sake (Is. 66:2, 5). Our prayers should be for the angel's message Daniel received after his fasting, prayer and repentance; Gabriel said, 'O Daniel, I am now come forth to give thee skill and understanding ... I am come to thee; for thou art greatly beloved: therefore understand the matter ...' (Dan. 9:21-23).

Angels of God come as fiery chariots and horses of fire

The Lord's powers and expressions are wonderfully complete and many times His Word refers to His holy angels. Psalm 104 describes some of God's powers and His angels: 'Who layeth the beams of his chambers in the waters: who maketh the clouds his chariot: who walketh upon the wings of the wind: Who maketh his angels spirits; his ministers a flaming fire' (Ps. 104:3-4). Scripture again confirmed the angels are made by God as 'his angels spirits, and his ministers a flame of fire' (Heb. 1:7). We can with confidence understand and visualize Elijah as he was taken up to heaven, without suffering earthly death; Elijah was carried in the hands of God's holy angels: 'There appeared a chariot of fire, and horses of fire, and parted them both asunder; and Elijah went up by a whirlwind into heaven' (2 Kgs. 2:11).

Open his eyes that he may see

Almost anyone who has been to church has heard: 'Fear not: for they that be with us are more than they that be with them' (2 Kgs. 6:16). A small army of Syrians had surrounded the house of Elisha and his servant in the city of Dothan. The Syrian force had been sent by their king to capture Elisha because he had repeatedly warned Israel beforehand about Syrians' military manoeuvres thwarting the king's planned military assaults. The king had been informed that Elisha had come to know the king's plans supernaturally by listening in the king's bed-chamber to the king's words. Elisha, as the doubly-anointed prophet of God who took up Elijah's prophetic mantle, had already seen exactly how God was providing complete protection. However, Elisha's servant did not have his eyes opened to see the spiritual beings protecting them. The servant was frightened and asked what they should do when the now famous 'fear not' statement by Elisha was made (2 Kgs. 6:8-16).

Elisha first asked God through prayer to 'open his servant's eyes, that he may see. And the Lord opened the eyes of the young man; and he saw: and, behold, the mountain was full of horses and chariots of fire round about Elisha' (2 Kgs. 6:16-17). The angels, upon the command of the Lord and after a prayerful request by Elisha, blinded all the Syrian troops. Scripture tells us that Elisha prayed to the Lord 'when they [the angelic hosts from heaven] came down to him' which was just after the servant described them 'round about Elisha' (2 Kgs. 6:17-18).

We should pray for our eyes to be opened whenever we find ourselves frightened by the sight of the host of enemy encamped around and ready to strike us. Although our eyes may not be opened to see the fiery angelic forces surrounding and protecting us, we must always trust the comforting Word of God because we are told: 'Fear not: for they that be with us are more than they that be with them.' 'And this is the confidence that we have in him, that, if we ask any thing according to his will, he heareth us: and if we know that he hear us, whatsoever we ask, we know that we have the petitions that we desired of him' (1 John 5:14-15).

The Cloud of the Lord and the Rebellious Israelites

The judgment of the Lord will surely come upon those who complain and ignore the ways of the Lord, especially after they have personally witnessed the will of the Lord. The cloud of the Lord appeared before His glory after the incident with Korah. Korah was a covetous priest who had a following of others who desired more power and glory for themselves. They wrongfully challenged the right of Moses and Aaron to represent the Lord to the people. The Lord openly displayed to all the people whom He chose as His representatives; His will was clear and unequivocal.

The Lord opened the earth which consumed Korah and all who followed him (including all of their property and homes) in their rebellion against the priesthood of Moses and Aaron.

> And the sons of Eliab; Nemuel, and Dathan, and Abiram. This is that Dathan and Abiram, which were famous in the congregation, who strove against Moses and against Aaron in the company of Korah, when they strove against the Lord.
> And the earth opened her mouth, and swallowed them up together with Korah, when that company died, what time the fire devoured two hundred and fifty men: and they became a sign.
> Notwithstanding the children of Korah died not
> (Num. 26:9-11).

After the Israelites witnessed this awesome demonstration the congregation of Israelites still 'murmured against Moses and against Aaron, saying, Ye have killed the people of the Lord' (Num. 16:41). And, this same congregation gathered against the chosen priests of God. As they looked toward the tabernacle of the congregation: 'the cloud covered it, and the glory of the Lord appeared' (Num. 16:42). God's wrath had promptly gone out from the Lord so He could consume the rebellious 'in a moment' (Num. 16:44-47). The people were saved from total destruction by God's wrath because of Moses' and Aaron's immediate atonement for the peoples' sin.

As the plague of the Lord rampantly swarmed over the people Aaron 'ran into the midst of the congregation' to make the saving atonement and 'he stood between the dead and the living; and the plague was stayed' (Num. 16:47-48). Because of the peoples' decision to continue to rebel against the will of the Lord and follow after Korah's rebellion with God's immediate punishment, fourteen thousand and seven hundred people died when God demonstrated His displeasure at the rebellion. 'Now all these things happened unto them for ensamples [as an example]: and they are written for our admonition, upon whom the ends of the world are come' (1 Cor. 10:11). Oh, the cloud that comes before the Lord's glory, may it always be as a blessing when we follow His will and not our own.

The Lord later also sent His angel to plague His people for the punishment of the sin of their King David. The sin of King David was his command to have a census of the people to be taken even after being warned by Joab, '... my lord the king, are they not all my lord's servants? why then doth my lord require this thing? why will he be a cause of trespass to Israel?' (1 Chron. 21:2-4). The answer to the prophet's question is given: 'And Satan stood up against Israel, and provoked David to number Israel' (1 Chron. 21:1). Because David repented 'unto God' of his sin and asked for God's wrath be brought upon himself instead of his people, David was allowed to choose the punishment: 'Thus saith the Lord, Choose thee Either three years' famine; or three months to be destroyed before thy foes, while that the sword of thine enemies overtaketh thee; or else three days the sword of the Lord, even the pestilence, in the land, and the angel of the Lord destroying throughout all the coasts of Israel' (1 Chron. 21:11-12).

David made his decision based upon the great mercies of the Lord and he chose to 'fall ... into the hand of the Lord' (1 Chron. 21:13). Just as God had done to the people after Korah's rebellion because of the peoples' murmuring, 'God sent an angel unto Jerusalem to destroy it' by sending pestilence upon Israel, 'and there fell of Israel seventy thousand men' (1 Chron. 21:14-15). When God told the angel: 'It is enough, stay now thine hand ... David lifted up his eyes, and saw the angel of the Lord stand between the earth and the heaven, having a drawn sword in his hand, stretched out over

Jerusalem. Then David and the elders of Israel, who were clothed in sackcloth, fell upon their faces' (1 Chron. 21:15-16). David's repentence before the Lord led to the plague being stayed from the people because David also honored God's Word through His prophet to buy certain land and 'built there an altar unto the Lord, and offered burnt offerings and peace offerings' (2 Sam. 24:17-25). The land David bought was on Mount Moriah where later his son Solomon would build the temple of the Lord, and where Abraham offered Isaac (2 Chron. 3:1; 1 Chron. 21:22-28; 22; see also Genesis 22:2).

Chapter 8

Angels Do Not Convict a Man's Heart

Jesus tells us of the Holy Comforter who comes to move men's hearts and minds toward the ways of Holy God:

> Nevertheless I tell you the truth; It is expedient for you that I go away: for if I go not away, the Comforter will not come unto you; but if I depart, I will send him unto you.
>
> And when he is come, he will reprove the world of sin, and of righteousness, and of judgment:
>
> Of sin, because they believe not on me;
>
> Of righteousness, because I go to my Father, ye see me no more;
>
> Of judgment because the prince of this world is judged.
>
> I have yet many things to say unto you, but ye cannot bear them now.
>
> Howbeit when he, the Spirit of truth, is come, he will guide you into all truth: for he shall not speak of himself; but whatsoever he shall hear, that shall he speak: and he will shew you things to come.
>
> He shall glorify me: for he shall receive of mine, and shall shew it unto you.
>
> All things that the Father hath are mine: therefore said I, that he shall take of mine, and shall shew it unto you (John 16:7-15).

Seek the Comforter, the Holy Spirit, who is God and who was promised by Jesus as the Person who will 'guide you in all truth' (John 16:13). Jesus teaches us to love Him:

If ye love me, keep my commandments.

And I will pray the Father, and he shall give you another Comforter, that he may abide with you for ever;

Even the Spirit of truth; whom the world cannot receive, because it seeth him not, neither knoweth him: but ye know him; for he dwelleth with you, and shall be in you.

I will not leave you comfortless: I will come to you (John 14:15-18).

As we can see from the above verses, the Holy Spirit is a person. 'He' is one of the persons of the Holy Trinity (Gen. 1:2, 26). One of the disciples asked: 'Lord, how is it that thou wilt manifest thyself unto us, and not unto the world?' (John 14:22). In response Jesus answered: 'If a man love me, he will keep my words: and **my Father will love him,** and we will come unto him, and **make our abode with him'** (John 14:23). Importantly, Christ explains, 'the Comforter, which is the Holy Ghost, whom the Father will send in my name, he shall teach you all things, and bring all things to your remembrance, whatsoever I have said unto you' (John 14:26).

The Holy Ghost is our Comforter and teacher of the truth
The Holy Spirit is called the Comforter (Greek: *paraclete*, as also in John 14:16, 26; 15:26; 16:7). In the root of this word are the ideas of advising, exhorting, comforting, strengthening, interceding and encouraging. The only other occurrence of this word outside the Gospel of John in the NT is in 1 John 2:1. It is applied to Christ and translated 'Advocate'. Here and in the other passages in John cited above, Christ teaches us that the Holy Spirit (1) will indwell Christians (John 14:16-17); (2) will help the disciples recall the events of His life (John 14:26); (3) will convict the world of sin, righteousness, and judgment (John 16:7-11); and, (4) will teach believers the truth (John 15:26; 16:13-15).

We should all rejoice in the promised gift of the indwelling Holy Ghost. He is truly a promised gift to each believer. Christ Jesus Himself teaches us this by promising the Comforter will be sent by the Father (John 14:16-17). Additionally, on the day of Pentecost Saint Peter proclaimed that Jesus was raised from the dead by God which was witnessed by himself and others. Peter continued teaching and proclaiming:

> Therefore [Jesus] being by the right hand of God exalted, and having received of the Father the promise of the Holy Ghost, he hath shed forth this, which ye now see and hear.
>
> Therefore let all the house of Israel know assuredly, that God hath made that same Jesus, whom ye have crucified, both Lord and Christ.
>
> Now when they [the men listening to Peter] heard this, they were pricked in their heart, and said unto Peter and to the rest of the apostles, Men and brethren, what shall we do?
>
> Then Peter said unto them, Repent, and be baptized every one of you in the name of Jesus Christ for the remission of sins, and ye shall receive the gift of the Holy Ghost.
>
> For the promise is unto you, and to your children, and to all that are afar off, even as many as the Lord our God shall call (Acts 2:32-33, 36, 37-39).

We therefore can truly rejoice because the gift of the Holy Ghost is a promised gift to all who believe, not a reward to some. The repentance Peter speaks above about is a call to change one's mind. Specifically, here, about Jesus of Nazareth, and to acknowledge Him as Lord (God) and Christ (Messiah) for it is repentance which brings salvation. All true repentance, even our repentance for specific sins committed after our salvation, is inspired by the Holy Spirit and always involves a 'godly sorrow' directing us back to our 'first love' who is Jesus Christ (2 Cor. 7:9-10; Rev. 2:4-5).

Angels study Gospel preaching and rejoice in heaven over each saved sinner

Peter desires us to understand that those who preach the Gospel 'with the Holy Ghost sent down from heaven' have another holy audience (1 Pet. 1:12). Even though the angels do not preach the Gospel 'the angels desire to look into' all things relating to the glory of the preaching and salvation brought by the Gospel of Jesus Christ (1 Pet. 1:12).

Angels can help us in our seeking for and living a righteous life in honour and respect for Jesus. He 'bare our sins in his own body on the tree, that we, being dead to sins, should live unto righteousness: by whose stripes ye were healed' (1 Pet. 2:24). Even though the angels in heaven rejoice over each sinner saved (Luke 15:10), we are cautioned to build ourselves up with 'holy faith, praying in the Holy Ghost, Keep yourselves in the love of God, looking for the mercy of our Lord Jesus Christ unto eternal life' (Jude 20-21). Only God the Father, Son and Spirit are worthy of our worship; never worship any creature because all were created by the Triune God (Rom. 1:24-25).

Chapter 9

Angels, When Seen, Glorify God

Eyes opened to see angels of God

Sometimes the comfort we receive from God may be from His messengers, the holy angels. Unless your eyes are opened to see the actions of the invisible forces of God you may never know if and when the angels are at your side, or surrounding your home, or fighting for the cause of God on your behalf.

Perhaps you may be fortunate on some occasion to have your eyes opened to see the invisible forces working around you daily. Scripture is replete with stories of those whose eyes were opened to the spiritual realm: (1) Elisha asked for his servant's eyes to be opened to see that those with them were more than those against them (2 Kgs. 6:16); (2) the eyes of Balaam's ass were opened to see the angel of the Lord blocking the path to destruction as were Balaam's eyes so opened (Num. 22:22, 31); and, (3) Jacob's eyes were opened to see the angels upon the ladder going up from earth to heaven's gate (Gen. 28:12).

Scripture tells us we should be striving by our thoughts and actions to love our brother who today is just a 'stranger'. Later in heaven we may discover the 'stranger' was an angel: 'Let brotherly love continue. Be not forgetful to entertain strangers: for thereby some have entertained angels unawares' (Heb. 13:1-2). Until our eyes are opened to the angels around us we must love everyone with a kind openness of heart.

Children's angels are always beholding our Father's face in heaven

Jesus teaches us that the angels of children actually sit in heaven before the throne of God always beholding the Father's face which is in heaven (Matt. 18:10). A recent event brings to life the stories in Scripture about our eyes being opened to see angels in the spiritual realm and the glory of the angels of children.

The following story from the previous year was told during 1999 television coverage of the most powerful tornados in the world's recorded history (winds exceeding three hundred miles per hour). The story was of a child who saw the protecting wings of a golden angel covering her and her family as they huddled in their bathroom. The child watched the covering angel as the rest of her family watched a Level 5 tornado tear the house away from around them. In the television story the mother described the wind being just a 'light breeze' and 'barely felt' by her or the other family members. The 1998 tornado winds recorded were above two hundred and fifty miles per hour! The mother watched the winds tear the tub away and be carried off. She watched the winds tear off the bathroom floor linoleum around where she and her children were huddled. The winds decimated the home around them. All of the other homes in the tornado's path were utterly destroyed as well. Neither the mother nor her 12-year old daughter saw the covering angelic being. But her young 4-year old child was granted the sight to see God's protecting angel who she described as extremely large, hovering directly over them, and shining of gold.

Chapter 10

Jesus Will Identify His Saints to Angels of God

Jesus warns us to fear God who has the power to cast us into hell and not to fear those that kill the body (Luke 12:4-5). God loves each individual and knows all in this world, 'even the very hairs on your head are all numbered,' and He knows when each sparrow falls to the ground (Matt. 10:29-30). Jesus will comfort one who believes in Him and so confesses with his mouth when He tells us: 'Fear not therefore: ye are of more value than many sparrows. Also I say unto you, Whosoever shall confess me before men, him shall the Son of man also confess before the angels of God: But he that denieth me before men shall be denied before the angels of God' (Luke 12:7-9). Jesus will confess only those whose names are found written in the book of life, and those whose names are not so written will be cast into the lake of fire (Rev. 20:15).

While the angels of God are hearing Jesus acknowledge His saints we can be assured and reassured 'the devil that deceived [the unbelieving][will be] cast into the lake of fire and brimstone, where the beast and the false prophet are, and shall be tormented day and night for ever and ever' (Rev. 20:10). Yet we are directed to share the Gospel of Christ Jesus with everyone we meet. Remember Revelation 20:11-15 describes the judgment of the unbelieving dead. This judgment occurs at the close of the Millennium and is 'the resurrection unto condemnation'. This judgment rests on works in order to show that punishment is deserved. God's judgment of the unbelieving will be His justice rolling on like a river, righteous like a never-ending stream (Amos 5:24). These unsaved people are primarily in this judgment because they rejected Christ as their Saviour during their lifetime (Rev. 20:12).

Without Christ as our mediator before God, the judgment will result in our being cast into the lake of fire. Jesus warns us all 'to fear him which is able to destroy both soul and body in hell' (Matt. 10:28). We must forsake our own knowledge and our personal prideful fame, and instead, we must become as children in order to understand the message of Jesus: 'I thank thee, O Father, Lord of heaven and earth, because thou hast hid these things from the wise and prudent, and hast revealed them unto babes' (Matt. 11:25). 'And Jesus called a little child unto him, and set him in the midst of them, And said, Verily I say unto you, Except ye be converted, and become as little children, ye shall not enter into the kingdom of heaven. Whosoever therefore shall humble himself as this little child, the same is greatest in the kingdom of heaven' (Matt. 18:2-4). Who hath ears to hear, let him hear because the promise is sure for everyone who accepts Jesus Christ as their Lord:

> Come unto me, all ye that labour and are heavy laden, and I will give you rest.
> Take my yoke upon you, and learn from me; for I am meek and lowly in heart: and ye shall find rest unto your souls.
> For my yoke is easy, and my burden is light (Matt. 11:28-30).

Seek always to understand the mysteries of the kingdom of heaven. Pray earnestly for understanding of the Word of God. 'The kingdom of heaven is like unto a net, that was cast into the sea, and gathered of every kind: Which, when it was full, they drew to shore, and sat down, and gathered the good into vessels, but cast the bad away. So shall it be at the end of the world: the angels shall come forth, and sever the wicked from among the just, And shall cast them into the furnace of fire: there shall be wailing and gnashing of teeth' (Matt. 13:47-50). 'Every plant, which my heavenly Father hath not planted, shall be rooted up' (Matt. 15:13). Our Lord asks: 'Are ye also yet without understanding?' (Matt. 15:16).

Jesus explains that He spoke to the people of the world in parables 'because they seeing see not; and hearing they hear not, neither do they understand' (Matt. 13:13). Jesus continues:

And in them is fulfilled the prophecy of Esaias, which saith, By hearing ye shall hear, and shall not understand; and seeing ye shall see, and shall not perceive.

For this people's heart is waxed gross, and their ears are dull of hearing, and their eyes they have closed; *lest at any time they should see with their eyes, and hear with their ears, and should understand with their heart, and should be converted, and I should heal them.*

But blessed are your eyes, for they see: and your ears, for they hear (Matt. 13:14-16).

Even though the angels of God will hear the heavenly confession of Jesus for His beloved saints, the angels make no judgment. Such judgment solely belongs to our Father through the authority given to His Son Jesus (Matt. 10:32-33; Heb. 12:23). The angels of God hear these confessions because of their royal place at the throne of God: 'Whosoever therefore shall confess me before men, him will I confess also before my Father which is in heaven. But whosoever shall deny me before men, him will I also deny before my Father which is in heaven' (Matt. 10:32-33). Angels do not want your worship which is for God alone.

Angels are brought to their greatest joy when they are doing all in their power to glorify the name of the Father. When the Son of man is seen coming in the clouds of heaven with power and great glory, 'he shall send his angels with a great sound of a trumpet, and they shall gather together his elect from the four winds, from one end of heaven to the other' (Matt. 24:30-31). After this gathering, the angels will witness the Father's greatest glory which is found in His Son Jesus when Jesus is glorifying His saints at God's throne in heaven. 'For the Son of man shall come in the glory of his Father with his angels; and then he shall reward every man according to his works' (Matt. 16:27). Each of these beloved saints in heaven establish the truth, mercy and love of the Father who promised to His Son Jesus from the foundations of time each of these saints (Matt. 25:34; Mark 10:40). The angels surrounding God's throne will surely sing out in loud praises and joy unspeakable by being present while the Father is glorified by Jesus' recognition and rewarding of His saints.

But to which of the angels said he [Jesus] at any time, Sit on my right hand, until I make thine enemies thy footstool?

Are they not all ministering spirits, sent forth to minister for them who shall be heirs of salvation? (Heb. 1:13-14)

For if the word spoken by angels was stedfast, and every transgression and disobedience received a just recompence of reward;

How shall we escape, if we neglect so great salvation; which at the first began to be spoken by the Lord, and was confirmed unto us by them that heard him (Heb. 2:2-3).

If you have not yet accepted Jesus as your Lord, while you are yet alive, you still have the hope of redemption because 'the Son of man is come to save that which was lost' (Matt. 18:11). After explaining the joy in the kingdom of heaven by the parable of a shepherd's rejoicing in finding one lost sheep from the otherwise safe flock, Jesus continues: 'It is not the will of your Father which is in heaven, that one of these little ones a child should perish' (Matt. 18:14).

Satan may tempt but may not enter the saints of Jesus

We are all born as children of wrath before faith brings us into the arms of Jesus (Eph. 2:3). In order to become a child of Satan we must make a choice to join the evil forces, with our goal the building of Satan's kingdom and opposing those who are children of God through their faith in Christ Jesus. We should shudder in fear and disgust at the thought of being embraced by Satan, but Scripture describes much of the world embracing evil. The Greek word in 1 John 5:19 describes the world in the arms of Satan which pictures a harlot in the arms of the one who has hired her. *A man's will must truly become perverted to turn from God's grace and love and make a conscious decision to wilfully bend to Satan's will.*

There are temptations from without upon the soul through the world (1 John 2:15-17); and, there are temptations from without upon the soul that come from Satan through the flesh. (1 Cor. 7:5). Even though there are temptations directly from Satan there is no possibility of the devil or his demons possessing the soul or body of one who has been born again. Remember, there is no fellowship between righteousness and unrighteousness; there is no communion between light and darkness; and, there is no agreement between the temple of God and idols (2 Cor. 6:14-16). Importantly, when you are born again of the Spirit your body becomes the temple of the Holy Spirit (1 Cor. 6:19).

Chapter 11

God's Angel Shall Go Before His People Protecting Them by Favour and Judgment

'God's Angel' or 'the Angel of the Lord' may be God Himself and not one of His created angels. The context of an angel's appearance and the exact language must be examined closely, with earnest prayer for understanding.

Abraham told his servant to follow certain directives from God and told him about Isaac's prospective bride: 'The Lord God of heaven, which took me from my father's house, and from the land of my kindred, and which spake unto me, and that sware unto me, saying, Unto thy seed will I give this land; he shall send his angel before thee, and thou shalt take a wife unto my son from hence. And if the woman will not be willing to follow thee, then thou shalt be clear from this my oath: only bring not my son thither again' (Gen. 24:7-8). Here, Abraham is comforted in knowing God's promise to send his angel before him guaranteeing no earthly interference.

The angel of God's presence either saves with mercy, or can become your enemy if you vex the Holy Spirit
We are taught, as was the house of Israel, it is important to confess our sins to God and always be motivated by our Father's love which inspires our honest confession to Him. Once we rebel we should not be surprised when God's mercy and protection are withdrawn leaving us open to Satan's demonic influences. Pray we always will be blessed by God's angel to save us.

I will mention the lovingkindnesses of the Lord, and the praises of the Lord, according to all that the Lord hath bestowed on us, and the great goodness toward the house of Israel, which he hath bestowed on them according to his mercies, and according to the multitude of his lovingkindnesses.

For he said, Surely they are my people, children that will not lie: so he was their Saviour.

In all their affliction he was afflicted, and the angel of his presence saved them: in his love and in his pity he redeemed them; and he bare them, and carried them all the days of old.

But they rebelled, and vexed his holy Spirit: therefore he was turned to be their enemy, and he fought against them (Is. 63: 7-10).

Serve the Lord your God and no other gods

While giving the 'law' to Moses, and particularly the laws relating to conquest, God makes the promise:

Behold, I send an Angel before thee, to keep thee in the way, and to bring thee into the place which I have prepared.

Beware of him, and obey his voice, provoke him not; for he will not pardon your transgressions: for my name is in him.

But if thou shalt indeed obey his voice, and do all that I speak; then I will be an enemy unto thine enemies, and an adversary unto thine adversaries.

For mine Angel shall go before thee, and bring thee in unto the Amorites, and the Hittites, and the Perizzites, and the Canaanites, the Hivites, and the Jebusites: and I will cut them off.

Thou shalt not bow down to their gods, nor serve them, nor do after their works: but thou shalt utterly overthrow them, and quite break down their images.

And ye shall serve the Lord your God, and he shall bless thy bread, and thy water; and I will take sickness away from the midst of thee (Exod. 23:20-25).

God's Angel can bring a blessing or a curse. God's Angel brought a curse because the people sinned a great sin by worshipping the golden calf when Moses tarried long with God. 'And Moses turned, and went down from the mount, and the two tables of the testimony [tablets of stone with the ten commandments] were in [Moses'] hand: the tables were written on both their sides ... **And the tables were**

the work of God, and the writing was the writing of God, graven upon the tables' (Exod. 32:15-16). At the same time God Himself was writing His laws for His chosen people, the people were creating and worshipping another god, the golden calf. Upon the discovery of the people's rebellion Moses' anger waxed hot, and he cast the tablets out of his hands, and broke them beneath the mount.

In Exodus 32 God's curse is brought upon the people:

> And it came to pass on the morrow, that Moses said unto the people, Ye have sinned a great sin: and now I will go up unto the Lord; peradventure I shall make an atonement for your sin.
>
> And Moses returned unto the Lord, and said, Oh, this people have sinned a great sin, and have made them gods of gold.
>
> Yet now, if thou wilt forgive their sin –; and if not, blot me, I pray thee, out of thy book which thou hast written.
>
> And the Lord said unto Moses, Whosoever hath sinned against me, him will I blot out of my book.
>
> Therefore now go, lead the people unto the place of which I have spoken unto thee: behold, mine Angel shall go before thee: nevertheless in the day when I visit I will visit their sin upon them.
>
> And the Lord plagued the people, because they made the calf, which Aaron made (Exod. 32:30-35).

Even after the people's open rebellion and sin, God promises Moses 'mine Angel shall go before thee' to drive out the other peoples of the land (Exod. 33:1-2). While the people sinned greatly by worshipping the golden calf: '... the Lord said unto Moses, I have seen this people, and, behold, it is a stiffnecked people: Now therefore let me alone, that my wrath may wax hot against them, and that I may consume them: and I will make of thee a great nation' (Exod. 32:9-10). Moses saved the people from God's total destruction by pleading with God to repent (change His mind) and not consume the people (Exod. 32:11-14).

Moses interceded for the people by pleading with God to '[r]emember Abraham, Isaac, and Israel, thy servants, to whom thou swarest by thine own self, and saidst unto them, I will multiply your seed as the stars of the heaven, and all this land that I have spoken of will I give unto your seed, and they shall inherit it for ever' (Exod.

32:13). Reading of the personal interchange brings great joy and wonder because God Himself was willing to speak to Moses intimately as a friend (Exod. 33:11).

The people did not completely escape God's wrath after their rebellion and sinfulness. As a parallel, even after our lives of rebellion and sinfulness we are given the opportunity to escape God's wrath by choosing to worship Jesus Christ as our Lord, so the people of Israel were given a similar opportunity. After their rebellious worship of other gods: '... Moses stood in the gate of the camp, and said, *Who is on the Lord's side? let him come unto me.* And all the sons of Levi gathered themselves together unto him. And he said unto them, Thus saith the Lord God of Israel, Put every man his sword by his side, and go in and out from gate to gate throughout the camp, and slay every man his brother, and every man his companion, and every man his neighbour. And the children of Levi did according to the word of Moses' (Exod. 32:26-28). On that day about three thousand men died of the sword because they did not repent of their sin and refused the offer to stand 'on the Lord's side' (Exod. 32:28).

Moses continued his intercession on behalf of his 'stiffnecked people' and continued his intimate relationship with the Lord who promised to protect the people by sending 'mine angel before thee'.

> And it came to pass, as Moses entered into the tabernacle, the cloudy pillar descended, and stood at the door of the tabernacle, and the Lord talked with Moses.
>
> And all the people saw the cloudy pillar stand at the tabernacle door: and all the people rose up and worshipped, every man in his tent door.
>
> *And the Lord spake unto Moses face to face, as a man speaketh unto his friend.* And he turned again into the camp: but his servant Joshua, the son of Nun, a young man, departed not out of the tabernacle (Exod. 33:9-11).

Moses continues to plead with God on behalf of his people, seeking the grace of God, and receiving from God His promise that: 'My presence shall go with thee, and I will give thee rest' because, as God explains: 'for thou hast found grace in my sight, and I know thee by name' (Exod. 33:14, 17).

The Angel of God, Joshua and Jericho

Another example of the blessing of the Angel of God going before His people is during the story of the battle of Jericho. Before the battle God appeared as a cloudy pillar at the tabernacle for intimate conversation with Moses. Joshua 'departed not out of the tabernacle' when God appeared. Thereafter, as Joshua readied himself for the battle:

> And it came to pass, when Joshua was by Jericho, that he lifted up his eyes and looked, and, behold, there stood a man over against him with his sword drawn in his hand: and Joshua went unto him, and said unto him, Art thou for us, or for our adversaries?
>
> And he said, Nay; but as captain of the host of the Lord am I now come. And Joshua fell on his face to the earth, and did worship, and said unto him, What saith my lord unto his servant?
>
> And the captain of the Lord's host said unto Joshua, Loose thy shoe from off thy foot; for the place whereon thou standest is holy. And Joshua did so (Josh. 5:13-15).
>
> Now Jericho was straitly shut up because of the children of Israel; none went out, and none came in.
>
> And the Lord said unto Joshua, See, I have given into thine hand Jericho, and the king thereof, and the mighty men of valour (Josh. 6:1-2)
>
> So the people shouted when the priest blew with the trumpets: and it came to pass, when the people heard the sound of the trumpet, and the people shouted with a great shout, that the wall fell down flat, so that the people went up into the city, every man straight before him, and they took the city (Josh. 6:20).

Note, in the above quoted Scripture that Joshua first worshipped the captain of the host of the Lord as Yahweh (Josh. 5:14). The 'Captain' angel did not correct Joshua about his worship probably because God was in fact present. God accepted Joshua's glorious worship from His servant. God's presence was also demonstrated when God told Joshua to take off his shoes because Joshua was on holy ground (Josh. 5:15). Scripture clearly shows that God Himself was the one to speak of the victory over Jericho (Josh. 6:2), using His force of angelic hosts and His chosen people, all for the glory of God.

The Angel of the Lord

'The Angel which redeemed me [Jacob renamed Israel by the angel] from all evil, bless the lads [Joseph's sons Manasseh and Ephraim]. ... And Israel said unto Joseph, Behold I die: but God shall be with you, and bring you again unto the land of your fathers' (Gen. 48:16, 21). The Angel of the Lord in the Old Testament willingly provided on behalf of God the requested blessing as promised of God; and the Angel could redeem these Saints from evil. 'Redeemed' in Hebrew is '*goel*' meaning 'to save' or 'to be a saviour or deliverer'. Goel is first used in the Bible when referring to the 'Angel'. Surely, this Angel was not a created being but rather was a preincarnate appearance of Christ Jesus, the second person of our Triune God. This Angel is more often referred to as 'the angel of the Lord'. At times this 'Angel' is a self-manifestation of God, usually speaking as God, and exercising the prerogatives of God. (See e.g. Genesis 16:7-14; 21:17-21; 22:11-18; 31:11, 13; 48:14-21; Exodus 3:2; Judges 2:1-4; 5:23; 6:11-24; 13:3-22; 2 Samuel 24:16; Zechariah 1:12; 3:1; 12:8).

Scripture repeatedly tells us the Lord says: 'I am the God of Abraham, Isaac, and Jacob.' (See e.g., Genesis 28:13; Exodus 3:2-6; Matthew 22:31-32; Luke 20:37-38). Abraham, the patriarch of every believer in Christ, on more than one occasion saw and spoke with the Angel of the Lord or with God Himself.

And when Abram was ninety years old and nine, the Lord appeared to Abram, and said unto him, I am the Almighty God; walk before me, and be thou perfect. And I will make my covenant between me and thee, and will multiply thee exceedingly.

And Abram fell on his face: and God talked with him, saying, As for me, behold my covenant is with thee, and thou shalt be a father of many nations.

Neither shall thy name any more be called Abram, but thy name shall be Abraham; for a father of many nations have I made thee (Gen. 17:1-4).

This visitation was probably the preincarnate Jesus, just as the next visitation was when the Lord came with two angels. It was in the plains of Mamre that Abraham was visited by Yahweh in physical form and the two angels; all ate and drank together (Gen. 18:1-8). Upon seeing the 'three men' standing by him, Abraham said, 'My Lord, if now I have found favour in thy sight, pass not away, I pray thee, from thy servant' (Gen. 18:2-3). The Incarnate Jesus, who supped with Abraham that day, for a third time gave Abraham and Sarah the good news of being blessed with a son the next year when He promised to return. (Gen. 18:10). In response to Sarah's laughter at the news of her conceiving a son the Lord God said: 'Is any thing too hard for the Lord? At the time appointed I will return unto thee, according to the time of life, and Sarah shall have a son' (Exod. 18:12-14).

God had directed Abraham to circumcise every man in the household as 'a token of the covenant betwixt me and you' (Gen. 17:11). Even the father of all Israel was a man who made mistakes. One of his greatest mistakes was agreeing with his wife Sarah when she persuaded him to sleep with her maid Hagar so a child might be born for the family inheritance. From that union Ishmael was born. It was not only Sarah who laughed at God's message of a son, Abraham also made that same mistake: 'Abraham fell upon his face, and laughed' at the news of God's blessing with a son from Sarai whom God had just renamed Sarah (Gen. 17:15-17).

At the news of a son to be from his wife, Abraham thought of seeking God's favour upon his son Ishmael: 'Abraham said unto God, O that Ishmael might live before thee!' (Gen. 17:18). In reply to Abraham's request for Ishmael to receive the inheritance, 'God said, Sarah thy wife shall bear thee a son indeed; and thou shalt call his name Isaac: and I will establish my covenant with him for an everlasting covenant, and with his seed after him. And as for Ishmael, I have heard thee: Behold, I have blessed him, and will make him fruitful, and will multiply him exceedingly; twelve princes shall he beget, and I will make him a great nation' (Gen. 17:19-20).

After blessing Ishmael in answer to Abraham's request of favour, God made clear that His 'covenant will I establish with Isaac, which Sarah shall bear unto thee at this set time in the next year' (Gen.

17:21). In all, the Lord personally and face-to-face told Abraham and/or Sarah on three occasions of the blessing of a son from Sarah's womb, yet on the first and last occasion Abraham and Sarah, respectively, laughed from their lack of faith. On the last occasion, Scripture clearly describes the Lord's appearance as that of a man, in the company of two other men. It appears the two men accompanying the Lord on this last occasion where the same two who appeared as angels to Lot at the gate of Sodom prior to that city's judgment. Abraham was blessed by seeing, speaking with, and supping with the Angel of the Lord.

Chapter 12

Do We Become Angels at Death?

Humans do not become angels at the moment of their death (1 Cor. 6:3; 13:1). Those chosen of God will surely be bodily resurrected. Even Job spoke of the resurrection: 'And though after my skin worms destroy this body, yet in my flesh shall I see God' (Job 19:26).

Luke 20:34-38 and Matthew 22:29-32 are set out below. With just a cursory reading of these two Scriptures one might conclude that those humans whom God resurrects from the dead become angels. A close reading, with sincere prayer, of the Word of God is always required to allow the Holy Spirit to help interpret the Word (Ps. 119:169). In both Luke and Matthew Jesus is giving an explanation to certain of the Sadducees who denied that there is any resurrection. Their question was about whose wife in heaven would be the woman who was the wife to seven brothers after each had died and finally the woman died herself. The question presented to Jesus was: 'Therefore in the resurrection whose wife of them is she? For seven had her to wife.'

Luke 20:35-36 explains Jesus' answer as:
'But they which shall be accounted worthy to obtain the world, and the resurrection from the dead, neither marry, nor are given in marriage: Neither can they die any more: for they are equal unto the angels; and are the children of God, being the children of the resurrection.'

Matthew 22:30 explains Jesus' answer as:
'For in the resurrection they neither marry, nor are given in marriage, but are as the angels of God in heaven.'

All too easily one might think the phrase 'as the angels of God' means that humans resurrected become angels. The point being made by Jesus is that angels do not produce offspring and neither do the resurrected saints procreate. The purpose of the resurrection is to enjoy the unique and special loving relationship between God, Jesus, the Holy Spirit, the resurrected saints, and the host of heavenly angels. Marriage relationships are no longer necessary for the family to grow in God's Word as they are in the world. Jesus goes on in both Gospels to explain the truth to the unbelieving Sadducees that in fact life is assured to those honoured by the resurrection.

Luke 20:37-38 explains Jesus' answer as:
Now that the dead are raised, even Moses shewed at the bush, when he calleth the Lord the God of Abraham, and the God of Isaac, and the God of Jacob. For he is not a God of the dead, but of the living: for all live unto him.

Matthew 22:31-32 explains Jesus' answer as:
But as touching the resurrection of the dead, have ye not read that which was spoken unto you by God, saying, I am the God of Abraham, and the God of Isaac, and the God of Jacob? God is not the God of the dead, but of the living.

Here, it is important to emphasize God's acknowledgment of a continuing relationship with Abraham, Isaac, and Jacob, though they had died long before. In Exodus 3:2-6 Moses turns to see the great sight of a burning bush that was not consumed. A flame of fire came out of its midst when God spoke: 'I am the God of thy father, the God of Abraham, the God of Isaac, and the God of Jacob. And Moses hid his face; for he was afraid to look upon God.' The message is the resurrected saints are alive as the angels are alive before the living God: 'for all live unto him.'

The bodily resurrection will not come immediately upon death. At our deaths we should be looking for angels who can appear as God's 'ministers a flaming fire' (Ps. 104:4). Believers should be comforted in knowing that at their earthly death that angels will surely be at their side to escort them through heaven's gate (Luke 16:22; Jude 9).

Spirits do not marry nor procreate

Jesus teaches that the worldly blessing of giving birth to children is no longer a part of the lives of the resurrected saints. They will continue to live just as the angels live while awaiting in heaven the bodily resurrection (Luke 20:35-36; Matt. 22:30).

Even though angels can physically manifest themselves, as they appear to be doing regularly according to the numerous angel encounter stories of today, they are referred to as 'ministering spirits' whose natural state is without a physical body (Heb. 1:14). As resurrected spirits we shall not marry nor reproduce after our earthly bodies die (Mark 12:25).

Chapter 13

Holy Angels are Meek in their Submission to God

Angels have had a multitude of time to demonstrate to God their pliability to His will, willingly submitting themselves to the correction of God. Angels' meek submission to God does not mean they are weak. In fact, the Scripture describes angels as powerful beings who are greater than man. All of the holy angels are humble whereas the rebellious angels who follow Satan are not. The rebellious angels are full of evil by their arrogant and proud ways.

In honour of God's name, the angels do everything under the Lord's will in heaven so His will shall be done in earth (Matt. 6:9-10). Angels, called God's hosts, are blessed by the Lord for they 'do His pleasure' acting as His 'ministers', 'excel[ling] in strength by doing his commandments, hearkening unto the voice of his word' (Ps. 103:19-21). The hosts of heaven are angels exalting God by praising the Lord (Ps. 148:2).

Angels were created to honour God and honour God's plan of redemption for the exalted destiny of Christians. We are made but 'a little lower than the angels' (Ps. 8:5). However, compare this same passage interpreted in NASB as 'a little lower than God'. Whether man was created a little lower than angels or a little lower than God, Scripture gives us a preview: Christians may become 'like angels in heaven' (Matt. 22:30). (For complete discussion of man's created stature see Chapter 15 entitled: 'Man made a little lower than the Angels? or, Made a little lower than the Triune God?')

Chapter 14

Who Is Above Angels?

Angels are far below the Christ Jesus whom God has appointed heir to all things and for whom all things of the worlds are created (Heb. 1:2). The angels of God worship Jesus who is called by God 'My Son' (Heb. 1:5-6).

God himself has told us that He 'maketh His angels spirits; His ministers a flaming of fire' (Ps. 104:4; Heb. 1:7). Angels, as well as the 'authorities and powers', have been made subject unto Jesus Christ 'who is gone into heaven, and is on the right hand of God' (1 Pet. 3:22). The heavens, inhabited by angels, 'declare the righteousness' of God the Lord (Ps. 97:6).

'And all the angels stood round about the throne, and about the elders and the four beasts, and fell before the throne on their faces, and worshipped God, Saying, Amen: Blessing, and glory, and wisdom, and thanksgiving, and honour, and power, and might, be unto our God for ever and ever. Amen' (Rev. 7:11-12).

And from Jesus Christ, who is the faithful witness, and the first begotten of the dead, and the prince of the kings of the earth. Unto him that loved us, and washed us from our sins in his own blood.

And hath made us kings and priests unto God and his Father; to him be glory and dominion for ever and ever. Amen.

Behold he cometh with clouds; and every eye shall see him, and they also which pierced him: and all kindreds of the earth shall wail because of him. Even so, Amen.

'I am the Alpha and Omega, the beginning and the ending, saith the Lord, which is, and which was, and which is to come, the Almighty' (Rev. 1:5-8).

In the Book of Revelation, John fell at Jesus' feet when Jesus said: 'Fear not; I am the first and the last: I am he that liveth, and was dead; and, behold, I am alive for evermore, Amen; and have the keys of hell and of death' (Rev. 1:17-18). The angels round about the throne of God, at the time of the opening of the Book of Life and loosening of the seven seals by Jesus, along with 'the beasts and the elders', will say with a loud voice: 'Worthy is the Lamb that was slain to receive power, and riches, and wisdom, and strength, and honour, and glory, and blessing'; and, every creature in heaven and on or under the earth will say: 'Blessing, and honour, and glory, and power, be unto him that sitteth upon the throne, and unto the Lamb for ever and ever' (Rev. 5:11-13). Jesus Christ's authority is above all angels and men, whether in heaven or on the earth.

Chapter 15

Man Made a Little Lower Than the Angels?
or,
Made a Little Lower Than the Triune God?

A brief discussion of the names of God is necessary to understand the conflict in interpretation of the Word regarding the place of man in creation. Specifically, the reference is to Psalm 8:5 wherein it states in the King James Version: 'For thou hast made him a little lower than the angels...' In the original Hebrew the word translated 'angels' is actually Elohim which is also one of the names of God.

God reveals Himself with almost four hundred names and specifically as Elohim or Jehovah. Both names are used with specific meaning and reference to the qualities of God. Elohim is the name of God used in matters of creation and power. Whereas, Jehovah is the name that is used in connection with all of His acts that lead to our redemption. Thus, in the account of the flood it is Elohim, the Creator, who tells Noah to enter the ark with two of each kind of animal for the preservation of the species; and, it is Jehovah, acting for redemption, who tells Noah to take seven of the clean animals for sacrifice, and who shuts him into the ark so he and his family will be safe.

Does the name Elohim mean God or angels?
It is interesting to note that Genesis 1:1 originally used the name Elohim in the statement: 'In the beginning God [Elohim] created the heaven and the earth.' The *Ryrie's Study Bible* note regarding this verse explains that Elohim here used is 'a generic term for deity as well as a proper name for the true God. It is used of pagan gods (Gen. 31:30; Exod. 12:12), angels (Ps. 8:5), men (Ps. 82:6), and judges (Exod.

21:6), though most frequently of the [one] true God. Its basic meaning is "strong one, mighty leader, supreme Deity". The form of the word is plural, indicating plentitude of power and majesty and allowing for the NT revelation of the triunity of the Godhead.'

Below are set out the pertinent verses in Psalm 8:

> What is man, that thou art mindful of him? and the son of man, that thou visited him? (v.4)
> *For thou hast made him a little lower than the angels,* and hast crowned him with glory and honour. (v.5)
> Thou madest him to have dominion over the works of thy hands; thou hast put all things under his feet: (v.6)
> All sheep and oxen, yea, and the beasts of the field. (v.7)
> The fowl of the air, and the fish of the sea, and whatsoever passeth through the paths of the seas (Ps. 8:4-8).

Interestingly, an enlightening Ryrie's note for Psalm 8:5 states: 'the angels (Heb., Elohim) is usually translated "God". The psalmist views man, created in God's image, as a little lower than God. In Hebrews 2:6-8, the passage is applied to Christ as Son of Man.'

This interpretation of God / Elohim instead of 'angels' *may* be more correct, especially when we consider that Scripture uses Elohim in reference to when God is acting as Creator. Thus, we find the original word for God, Elohim, being translated as angels in the King James Version. However, would the translation be more correct if the word was translated 'God': 'man was made a little lower than God' in Psalm 8 and 'Jesus, who was made a little lower than God for the suffering of death' in Hebrew 2:9?

Below are set out the pertinent verses in Hebrews:

> For unto the angels hath he not put in subjection the world to come, whereof we speak (v.5).
> But one in a certain place testified, saying, [the quoting of Psalm 8 begins] What is man, that thou art mindful of him? or the son of man, that thou visited him? (v.6)
> Thou madest him a little lower than the angels; thou crownedst him with glory and honour, and didst set him over the works of thy hands: (v.7)

Thou has put all things in subjection under his feet. For in that he put all in subjection under him, he left nothing that is not put under him. [end quoting Psalm 8] But now we see not yet all things put under him (v.8).

But we see Jesus, who was made a little lower than the angels for the suffering of death, crowned with glory and honour; that he by the grace of God should taste death for every man (Heb. 2:5-9).

Ryrie's note for Hebrews 2:7 goes back to the interpretation that man was created a little lower than angels and states specifically: 'a little lower. This may mean (1) for a short time, or (2) more likely a little lower in rank. In the order of creation, man is lower than angels, and, in the Incarnation, Christ took this lower place.'

To compare, Scripture tells us of Jesus: 'For verily he took not on him the nature of angels; but he took on him the seed of Abraham. Wherefore in all things it behoved him to be made like unto his brethren, that he might be a merciful and faithful high priest in things pertaining to God, to make reconciliation for the sins of the people. For in that he himself hath suffered being tempted, he is able to succour them that are tempted' (Heb. 2:16-18).

Man was created sinless and in fellowship with God

Both Psalm 8 and its repeated verses in Hebrews refer to when man was created. At the creation of Adam and Eve they walked with God in the Garden of Eden in perfect fellowship. Angels are not referred to in Scripture as ever 'walking with God in fellowship'. Also, angels are created beings that do not die and will live forever into eternity. Holy angels will live forever in the presence of God; while the fallen angels will live imprisoned and separated from God, in eternal punishment. In fact, hell was created for Satan and his fallen angels and not for man (Matt. 25:41).

On the sixth day Elohim God decided to create man in 'our image, after our likeness' (Gen. 1:26). In the fifth chapter of Genesis we read a summary of the creation of man: 'In the day that God created man, in the likeness of God made he him; male and female created he them; and blessed them, and called their name Adam, in the day when they were created' (Gen. 5:1, 2). Man was given by God authority over everything: 'Be fruitful, and multiply, and replenish the earth, and subject it; and have dominion over the fish of the sea, and over the fowl of the air, and over every living thing that moveth upon the earth' (Gen. 1:28).

As he was made in the image of God, in the image of Triune God, man was absolutely made above every angel; and, by being given dominion over the earth man was made above Satan who had been given originally that dominion upon God's creation (Ezek. 28:14). When we discover that in the original Hebrew and Greek in Psalm 8 and Hebrews, respectively, the word used is *Elohim* and not angels, the evidence seems strong that man was in fact made 'a little lower than God'. The question we should be asking with this interpretation, which seems to glorify man the creature, instead of God the Creator, is whether such an interpretation is inspired of the Holy Spirit or the spirit of human pride?

Man made a little lower than angels: fits overall plan of Satan eating dust?

God's overall plan of dealing with Satan's deception of Adam and Eve in the Garden of Eden is to assure Satan is ever eating dust. Psalm 8:5 and Hebrews 2:7 traditional interpretation of *Elohim* as the word 'angels' appears to have been used because this interpretation fits well into the overall plan of God to assure Satan eats dust (Gen. 3:14-15). The key phrase in the passages is that which places man in the scheme of creation as being made 'lower than the angels'.

Here is the divine strategy: Out of the lowest, God shall bring the highest. In the Old Testament the Lord says He has 'respect unto the lowly: but the proud he knoweth afar off' (Ps. 138:6). In the New Testament Jesus says I am 'meek and lowly in heart' (Matt. 11:29). St. Paul further explains God's mysterious plan:

> Because the foolishness of God is wiser than men; and the weakness of God is stronger than men.
>
> For ye see your calling, brethren, how that not many wise men after the flesh, not many mighty, not many noble, are called:
>
> But God hath chosen the foolish things of the world to confound the wise; and God hath chosen the weak things of the world to confound the things which are mighty;

And base things of the world, and things which are despised, hath God chosen, yea, and things which are not, to bring to nought things that are:

That no flesh should glory in his presence.

But of him are ye in Christ Jesus, who of God is made unto us wisdom, and righteousness, and sanctification, and redemption:

That, according as it is written, He that glorieth, let him glory in the Lord (1 Cor. 1:25-30).

He shall even, Himself, condescend to be Incarnate in this low level of creation; and Christ Himself willingly became a 'curse for us: for it is written, Cursed is every one that hangeth on a tree' (Gal. 3:13). And out of that level of curses, even out of the level man had fallen to, God shall bring a race of sons who shall be raised to live in fellowship with Him forever in the government of the universe (Eph. 2:5-6). Thus shall come the greatest glory of God, and the full victory in the punishment of Satan's prideful heart.

Man was truly a new thing and not created after the order of angels which are called by their names: angels, seraphims, cherubims, and rightfully called principalities and powers. The angels of the lowest status have greater powers than man who is tied by the laws of nature, including being tied to earth by gravity. The use by the Holy Spirit of Psalm 8 to describe Jesus' created position on earth appears to clearly highlight the correct interpretation of both of Psalm 8 and Hebrews' reference to the being created 'a little lower than ...' Even though the RSV translates the passage in the Psalms, 'Thou hast made him little less than God', but in the New Testament quotation of this passage, found in chapter 2 of Hebrews, is 'Thou didst make him [Jesus], for a little while, lower than the angels'.

The New Testament translation, based upon the context of Jesus' mission and purpose and means, along with the quotation from Psalm 8, seems sufficient to justify the teaching: in being made for a little while lower than the angels, He was, indeed, made lower than the angels. Angels do not die in the physical sense but in the spiritual sense they can die by being separated from God – they live for eternity as spirits, either with God or in the fiery pit. Jesus was born to die in agreement with His Father's will. By agreeing to submit to death Jesus was born a little below the angels, at least for a brief time.

Jesus came to serve through humility and die

St. Paul explains why both passages should be interpreted that man and Jesus were made a little lower than angels, if there is doubt:

> Let this mind be in you, which was also in Christ Jesus:
> Who, being in the form of God, thought it not robbery to be equal with God:
> But made himself of no reputation, and took upon him the form of a servant, and was made in the likeness of men:
> And being found in fashion as a man, he humbled himself, and became obedient unto death, even the death of the cross.
> Wherefore God also hath highly exalted him, and given him a name which is above every name:
> That at the name of Jesus every knee should bow, of things in heaven, and things in earth, and things under the earth;
> And that every tongue should confess that Jesus Christ is Lord, to the glory of God the Father (Phil. 2:5-11).

The interpretation of these two Scriptural passages in Psalm 8 and Hebrews 2 must be by the power of the Spirit, as all spiritual truth comes. Therefore we must seek to understand this mystery by praying earnestly for divine revelation (1 Cor. 2:9-13). Come to God asking to be His servant, of no personal reputation, and He will surely provide the spiritual guidance to understand the essence of these Scriptures, and all Scripture.

What is the image of God separating man from the angels?

When man was made he was endowed with something called 'the image of God'. Since 'God is spirit' (John 4:24) and 'a spirit hath not flesh and bones' (Luke 24:39) what are we to make of the Scriptures using figures of speech describing God using the bodily characteristics of man? For example: 'The eyes of the Lord run to and fro throughout the whole earth ... (2 Chron. 16:9); and, 'The Lord's hand is not shortened, that it cannot save; neither his ear heavy, that it cannot hear' (Is. 59:1). Should we then conclude the image of God is as the physical make-up of man? Probably not, especially considering that we are also told of God: 'He shall cover thee with his feathers, and under his wings shalt thou trust' (Ps. 91:4).

God knows the beginning from the end and is outside of time watching all and knowing all. With God's omniscience (all knowledge) He has always been aware of the form His only begotten Son would take when He came as a man to dwell here on earth. 'Who is the image of the invisible God, the firstborn of every creature. And he is the head of the body, the church: who is the beginning, the firstborn from the dead; that in all things he might have pre-eminence' (Col. 1:15, 18). Our perfection, even as Adam and Eve's perfection upon their creation, is preached to all men, 'warning every man, and teaching every man in all wisdom; that we may present every man perfect in Christ Jesus' (Col. 1:29).

As Jesus took man's form, 'made in the image of God', we can more easily understand the expressions using our physical form to describe God's invisible spiritual functions: eyes that see by comprehending the light yet seeing nothing in darkness, as God created the light because He is light, in Him is no darkness at all (1 John 1:5) and in essence God's awareness of all things; arms and hands that control and form the earth around about, as God's ability to form all things as He would desire with His indescribable power and strength. The physical manifestation of man is crucially important to God for He commanded the institution of the death penalty on murderers because He made man in His image (Gen. 9:6).

Scripture teaches that mere flesh and blood cannot inherit the kingdom of God (1 Cor. 15:50). The 'divine' image of God surely departed with the fall of Adam and all his descendants lack any such 'divine' image. Today, the almost universal humanistic viewpoint teaches and embraces the New Age theory that man, in his present condition, is naturally good and is equal to God because man is the only god he can ever truly know (sic). The Bible teaches of the rebellious nature of New Age vanity with its prideful desires of godhood. Since Adam's fall when his children were begat 'in his own likeness, after his image' any chance of being born in the divine image of God has been impossible (Gen. 5:3). *Unless a man is born again from God through the Spirit by faith in Jesus Christ, who is the Word* (John 1:1, 2, 14), *that man cannot enter the kingdom of God* (John 3:3, 5, 6). *'For God, who commanded the light to shine out of darkness, hath shined in our hearts, to give the light of the knowledge of the glory of God in the face of Jesus Christ'* (2 Cor. 4:6).

The Bible also makes clear that man, following his fall, has been void of the spiritual image of God. After Adam's fall from grace man's image is now far, so very far, from the image of God in which the first humans were created in Paradise. Presently, we are born 'dead in trespasses and sins' (Eph. 2:1); and, we are 'not subject to the law of God, neither indeed can be' (Rom. 8:7) I know that in my flesh 'dwelleth no good thing: for to will is present in me; but how to perform that which is good I find not' (Rom. 7:18), always finding myself captive to the law of sin which is in my members (Rom. 7:23). Contrary to the Antichristian teaching of the New Age we have the future hope after our natural birth of a new spiritual birth. Our new spiritual birth through Jesus comes with the knowledge that 'as we have borne the image of the earthy, we shall also bear the image of the heavenly' (1 Cor. 15:49). We trust in the promise that through our faith in Christ Jesus and His redemptive death and resurrection we, as individual believers, will become partakers of the divine nature (2 Pet. 1:4; John 5:24).

Before the fall of Adam and Eve, our 'first parents', they were truly spiritual beings because they were indwelt with God's Holy Spirit. Upon our rebirth through faith in Jesus we are promised to again be made whole. After His resurrection Jesus first appeared suddenly to the frightened apostles in the upper room. They had not yet understood the wonderful meaning of His death on the cross as their Messiah. Jesus spoke to them and Jesus 'breathed on them', and said to them, 'Receive ye the Holy Spirit ...' (John 20:22). The risen Lord Jesus Christ had returned to proclaim His victory of life over death after He accomplished His mission of redemption for fallen man. He began His work among His disciples by breathing on to them the Holy Spirit, for man could once more be made in the image of God, if he would believe and obey Jesus. All believers could now trust they were newly formed: having 'put on the new man, which is renewed in knowledge after the image of him that created him' (Col. 3:10).

The Holy Spirit was earlier in the Bible spoken of when: 'The Lord God formed man of the dust of the ground, and breathed into his nostrils the breath of life; and man became a living soul' (Gen.

2:7). The image of God came into Adam by the divine inbreathing of the breath of God. That divine image was lost in the fall.

Man was first created with a knowledge and a moral righteousness that were in the image of God. However, due to one man's rebellious will sin entered all men and sin remains in all of us. Even though man was created on a low plane, lower than the angels in power and might and beauty, man was first created as God intended for all His sons. We should pray for our wills to be as God's will by becoming 'children of God' through a spiritual rebirth by faith in Jesus (Gal. 3:26). Those who adopt the New Age humanist religion trust in themselves; they have declared themselves the 'children of wrath' (Eph. 2:3); or, they have declared themselves the children of the devil (John 8:44).

Without faith in Jesus only the fool would deny 'the heart is deceitful above all things, and incurably sick' (Jer. 17:9). Pray to enter 'God's rest', always forsaking 'an evil heart of unbelief, in departing from the living God' (Heb. 3:12). The devil and his horde of demons are united as the 'world' to oppose the course of all believers (John 15:18-19) who always should be praying for the promised protection of the heavenly host of holy angels.

Angels seek to understand the image of God due to indwelling Spirit of Christ

Jesus warned that hell would be 'outer darkness' for those who trust in themselves and deny God's will; and, those who refuse His offer of salvation 'will be cast out into outer darkness' (Matt. 8:12; 22:13) with the terrible image of eternal separation from God and man. Those suffering the separation of hell will do it with the remorse of knowing they had the opportunity to come into heaven with God but refused. All who reject God choose to follow Satan into hell where there is no exit and no second chance. Even though the end is already known by the teaching of Scripture, man must choose between three possible sources of hope: God, man or the devil. 'For the earth shall be filled with the knowledge of the glory of the Lord, as the waters cover the sea' (Hab. 2:14). Let the angels rejoice as we bring others to the knowledge of the saving grace of Jesus before it is too late.

By choosing to worship Christ we will have the opportunity and capacity to comprehend certain spiritual realities – 'wisdom and prudence' the known 'mystery of [Christ's] will' – angels cannot understand (Eph. 1:8-10; 3:10). Angels are seeking to understand the mystery of the indwelling Spirit of Christ (1 Pet. 1:12). After our death and resurrection with Christ His believers will be assigned as 'judges' (leaders) and teachers of the angels (Dan. 7:18-27; 1 Cor. 6:2-3).

Chapter 16

Archangels Always Sent by the Call of the Lord

Archangels are angels of exalted rank and power who are sent by God to carry out special assignments and deliver special messages. The Greek word for archangels is '*archangelos*'.

Angel Gabriel's name means either 'man of God' or 'hero of God', and his ministry involves making special announcements concerning God's plans (Dan. 8:16; 9:21). He and Michael, the archangel, are the only angels named in the Bible. Michael is described as 'The great prince who stands watch over the sons of [God's] people' (Dan. 12:1). Michael's very name means 'Who is like God?' And thus Michael is always doing His bidding and honouring His holy name.

The angel Gabriel (an archangel?) is clothed in glory described in Daniel 10:5-6: 'Then I lifted up mine eyes, and looked, and behold a certain man clothed in linen, whose loins were girded with fine gold of Uphaz: His body also was like the beryl [blue green or turquoise], and his face as the appearance of lightening, and his eyes as lamps of fire, and his arms and his feet like in colour to polished brass, and the voice of his words like the voice of a multitude.'

The Lord's archangels team together to carry out the will of God. They fight the good fight against the evils of this world. They must team together to fight off the evil princes who are allowed to rule over the world's kingdoms. The Bible tells of how Gabriel was sent by God to immediately answer the prayers of Daniel but was held up for twenty-one days by the Prince of Persia until Michael came to help (Dan. 10:12-14). With the help of Michael the Prince of Persia was defeated for the time to allow Gabriel to bring his message to Daniel. Gabriel shares with us that after giving his message both he and Michael would return to fight against the Princes of Persia and Greece (Dan. 10:12-21).

Gabriel and Michael are not willing, nor presumptuous, to fight the devil himself and instead rely upon the Word of God. Why is this so? The devil is of higher authority than the archangels; and they respect this authority because all authority is given by God himself.

The angels of God are spirits and know of spiritual matters when it comes to respecting God's authority, as compared to the men of this world who speak evil of those things which they know not. Just as the mockers of the last days walk after their own ungodly lusts, only 'filthy dreamers defile the flesh, despise dominion, and speak evil of dignities' (Jude 8-10). We should be warned that if the Lord's archangels respect the devil we should show the same respect. Whether the Apostle Peter in 2 Peter 2 is referring to evil angels or the worldly false teachers, we are cautioned to realize that if holy angels of great power limit their words of accusation, then mere mortal men should also be so cautioned to hold their evil tongues concerning spiritual matters:

> But there were false prophets also among the people, even as there shall be false teachers among you, who privily shall bring in damnable heresies, even denying the Lord that bought them, and bring upon themselves swift destruction.
>
> And many shall follow their pernicious ways; by reason of whom the way of truth shall be evil spoken of.
>
> And through covetousness shall they with feigned words make merchandise of you: whose judgment now of a long time lingereth not, and their damnation slumbereth not.
>
> For if God spared not the angels that sinned, but cast them down to hell, and delivered them into chains of darkness, to be reserved unto judgment;
>
> And spared not the old world, but saved Noah the eighth person, a preacher of righteousness, bringing in the flood upon the world of the ungodly (2 Pet. 2:1-5).
>
> And delivered just Lot, vexed with the filthy conversation of the wicked;
>
> (For that righteous man dwelling among them, in seeing and hearing vexed his righteous soul from day to day with their unlawful deeds;)

The Lord knoweth how to deliver the godly out of temptations, and to reserve the unjust unto the day of judgment to be punished:

But chiefly them that walk after the flesh in the lust of uncleanness, and despise government. Presumptuous are they, selfwilled, they are not afraid to speak evil of dignities.

Whereas angels, which are greater in power and might, bring not railing accusation against them before the Lord.

But these, as natural brute beasts, made to be taken and destroyed, speak evil of the things that they understand not; and shall utterly perish in their own corruption (2 Pet. 2:7-12).

For when they speak great swelling words of vanity, they allure through the lusts of the flesh, through much wantonness those that were clean escaped from them who live in error (2 Pet. 2:18)

For if after they have escaped the pollutions of the world through the knowledge of the Lord and Saviour Jesus Christ, they are again entangled therein, and overcome, the latter end is worse with them than the beginning (2 Pet. 2:20).

Satan is rebuked by the Word of God or by God Himself

Therefore, answer the devil as Michael did in Jude 9 while contending over the body of Moses. Michael dared not bring against him a railing accusation but said, 'The Lord rebuke thee'. Be warned my friend, even Christ Jesus answered the temptations of the devil with the Word of God: 'It is written, Man shall not live by bread alone, but by every word that proceedeth out of the mouth of God.. It is written again, Thou shalt not tempt the Lord thy God... Get thee hence, Satan: for it is written, Thou shalt worship the Lord thy God, and him only shalt thou serve' (Matt. 4:4, 7, 10). Too often when we hear this story of Satan being rebuked we forget the next verse: 'Then the devil leaveth him, and, behold, angels came and ministered unto him' (Matt. 4:11).

Six days before Jesus took Peter, John and James (John's brother) up into a high mountain where Jesus was transfigured before them, we are told in God's Word that when Satan spoke through Peter Jesus rebuked him:

Then charged he his disciples that they should tell no man that he was Jesus the Christ. From that time forth began Jesus to shew unto his disciples, how that he must go unto Jerusalem, and suffer many things of the elders and chief priests and scribes, and be killed, and be raised again the third day.

Then Peter took him, saying, Be it far from thee, Lord: this shall not be unto thee.

But he turned, and said unto Peter, Get thee behind me, Satan: thou art an offence unto me: for thou savourest not the things that be of God, but those that be of men.

Then said Jesus unto his disciples, If any man will come after me, let him deny himself, and take up his cross, and follow me.

For whosoever will save his life shall lose it: and whosoever will lose his life for my sake shall find it.

For what is a man profited, if he shall gain the whole world, and lose his own soul? or what shall a man give in exchange for his soul?

For the Son of man shall come in the glory of his Father with his angels; and then he shall reward every man according to his works.

Verily I say unto you, There be some standing here, which shall not taste of death, till they see the Son of man coming in his kingdom (Matt. 16:20-28).

We should strive to have our lives right with God as we daily look for Jesus' coming with His angels in the glory of His Father. Make the decision today to follow Jesus as your Lord and Saviour, learn to deny yourself and take up the cross, savour the things of God and always answer Satan with the sword of the Word of God.

God's great favour spoken by archangel Gabriel

If ever visited by the angel Gabriel you may be glad of your favour of God. Zacharias, Mary, and Daniel were favoured by God and visited. While Daniel was praying Gabriel flew to him, touching him and speaking with him. Gabriel's purpose was to give to Daniel skill and understanding. Gabriel said he was there to explain Daniel's vision because Daniel was 'greatly beloved' (Dan. 9:21-22). Daniel was visited more than once by Gabriel who had the appearance of a man and yet was directed by a man's voice to 'make this man to understand the vision' (Dan. 8:15-16; 9:21).

Can we ever forget angel Gabriel's famous message to Mary:

Hail, thou that are highly favoured, the Lord is with thee: blessed art thou among women (Luke 1: 28).

Fear not, Mary: for thou hast found favour with God.
And, behold thou shalt conceive in thy womb, and bring forth a son, and shalt call his name JESUS.
He shall be great, and shall be called the Son of the Highest: and the Lord God shall give unto him the throne of his father David: And he shall reign over the house of Jacob for ever; and of his kingdom there shall be no end (Luke 1:30-33).

The Holy Ghost shall come upon thee, and the power of the Highest shall over-shadow thee: therefore also that holy thing which shall be born of thee shall be called the Son of God (Luke 1:35).

'For with God nothing shall be impossible' (Luke 1:37). These words of angel Gabriel to Mary should bring comfort to everyone who calls upon the Lord.

The strength of the Lord shall mount us up with wings as eagles
You can be assured that God 'shall give his angels charge over thee, to keep thee in all thy ways' so long as you 'dwell in the secret place of the most High' and 'say of the Lord, He is my refuge and my fortress: my God; in him will I trust' (Ps. 91:11, 1-2). By seeking the spiritual kingdom of God through the saving grace of his only begotten Son Jesus Christ who died for the sins of the world we can be secure as we walk through the shadow of death in the world of today (John 3:16; Ps. 23). Fear not and fear no evil because the Lord is your strength (Ps. 23 and 27). Trust in Jesus who came to defeat the devil 'for the devil sinneth from the beginning' and 'for this purpose the Son of God was manifested, that he might destroy the works of the devil' (1 John 3:8-9). God's archangel Michael is described as, 'The great prince who stands watch over the sons of [God's] people' (Dan. 12:1).

Only those called 'sons of God' have the unbridled joy of knowing the love bestowed by the Father because we not only perceive, but trust through faith that God himself, through his only begotten Son, laid down his life for us (1 John 3:1, 16). Angels of the Lord will minister to those who keep the Father's commandment that 'we should believe on the name of his Son Jesus Christ, and love one another' (1 John 3:23).

The foretelling of John the Baptist is revealed as the preparer of the way for the Lord Jesus, as was the strength of the Lord revealed by the prophet Isaiah:

The voice of him [John the Baptist] that crieth in the wilderness, Prepare ye the way of the Lord, make straight in the desert a highway for our God. Every valley shall be exalted, and every mountain and hill shall be made low: and the crooked shall be made straight, and the rough places plain: And the glory of the Lord shall be revealed, and all flesh shall see it together: for the mouth of the Lord hath spoken it (Is. 40:3-5).

The grass withereth, the flower fadeth: but the word of our God shall stand for ever (Is. 40:8).

Behold, the Lord God will come with strong hand, and his arm shall rule for him: behold, his reward is with him, and his work before him. He shall feed his flock like a shepherd: he shall gather the lambs with his arm, and carry them in his bosom, and shall gently lead those that are with young (Is. 40:10-11).

Who hath directed the Spirit of the Lord, or being his counsellor hath taught him?

Behold, the nations are as a drop of a bucket, and are counted as the small dust of the balance: behold, he taketh up the isles as a very little thing. ... All nations before him are as nothing; and they are counted to him less than nothing, and vanity.

The grass witherest, the flower fadeth: but the word of our God shall stand for ever (Is. 40:13, 15; 17:8).

Have ye not known? have ye not heard? hath it not been told you from the beginning? have ye not understood from the foundations of the earth? It is he that sitteth upon the circle of the earth, and the inhabitants thereof are as grasshoppers; that stretcheth out the heavens as a curtain, and spreadeth them out as a tent to dwell in: That bringeth the princes to nothing; he maketh the judges of the earth as vanity (Isaiah 40:21-23).

To whom then will ye liken me, or shall I be equal? saith the Holy One. Lift up your eyes on high, and behold who hath created these things, that bringeth out their host by number: he calleth them all by names by the greatness of his might, for that he is strong in power; not one faileth (Is. 40:25-26).

Hast thou not known? hast thou not heard, that the everlasting God, the Lord, the Creator of the ends of the earth, fainteth not, neither is weary? there is no searching of his understanding (Is. 40:28).

But they that wait upon the Lord shall renew their strength; they shall mount up with wings as eagles; they shall run, and not be weary; and they shall walk, and not faint (Is. 40:31).

Love God with all of your heart, mind and soul with full assurance that such love means you 'dwell in the secret place of the most High' and thus 'shall abide under the shadow of the Almighty' (Ps. 91:1). God does not faint and does not weary in His love, power and comfort for those who trust in Him, even as the shadow of death may appear to overcome God's light:

The Lord is my shepherd; I shall not want. He maketh me to lie down in green pastures: he leadeth me beside the still waters. He restoreth my soul: he leadeth me in the paths of righteousness for his name's sake.

Yea, though I walk through the valley of the shadow of death, I will fear no evil: for thou art with me; thy rod and thy staff they comfort me.

Thou preparest a table before me in the presence of mine enemies: thou anointest my head with oil; my cup runneth over.

Surely goodness and mercy shall follow me all the days of my life: and I will dwell in the house of the Lord for ever (Ps. 23:1-6).

The children of the devil 'do not righteousness' and are 'not of God, neither he that loveth not his brother' (1 John 3:10). However, do not let Satan deceive you if a time comes when you find, as Paul did, 'a thorn in the flesh' because you should understand that thorn just may be 'the messenger of Satan to buffet you lest you should be exalted above measure' (2 Cor. 12:7). If you pray to God for relief from your 'thorn in the flesh' your answer might be the same Paul heard from Jesus: 'My grace is sufficient for thee: for my strength is made perfect in weakness.' But they that wait upon the Lord shall renew their strength; they shall mount up with wings as eagles, not be weary, and not faint. The wings as eagles are the angels of the Lord who renew our strength in the face of evil, even the shadow of death.

Chapter 17

God's Use of Living Creatures – by His Holy Angels?

Quails of the Lord: be careful of your desires

Was the wind of the Lord as described in Numbers 11:31 His holy angels who flew through the air directing and pushing the quails to the people from the sea? Was it holy angels who took action upon the word of the Lord glorifying the name of the Lord? For when Moses questioned how he was to provide such a huge bounty of meat for all of the hundreds of thousands to eat, the Lord answered: 'Is the Lord's hand waxed short? thou shalt see now whether my word shall come to pass unto thee or not... And there went forth a wind from the Lord, and brought quails from the sea, and let them fall by the camp...' (Num. 11:21-23, 31).

What was the setting for God's supernatural provision for the people of Israel? Look to see if the wind of the Lord caused by the word of the Lord was moved by the wings of the Lord's holy angels. Or, was the word of the Lord displayed by the wind 'the fierceness of his anger, wrath, and indignation, and trouble, by sending evil angels among them' as described in Psalm 78:49?

God heard the prayers of intercession from Moses at Taberah, which in Hebrew means 'burning'. The land was named Taberah because 'when the people complained, it displeased the Lord; and the Lord heard it; and his anger was kindled; and the fire of the Lord burnt among them, and consumed them that were in the uttermost parts of the camp (Num. 11:1-2). The book of Numbers does not tell us whether the judgment of fire extended only to the tents on the outskirts of the camp or to people or (most likely) to both. Scripture does not refer to the Israel people giving thanks to the Lord who

119

instead complained and murmered against the plight they suffered as they continued their travels towards the promised land. The people encamped after they had followed the 'cloud of the Lord' for eleven months in the Sinai and around the land of Moab.

Scripture tells us that just before the people 'complained', the Lord had protected His people from all enemies: 'when it the ark set forward, Moses said, Rise up, Lord, and let thine enemies be scattered; and let them that hate thee flee before thee. And when it rested, he said, Return, O Lord, unto the many thousands of Israel' (Num. 10:35-36).

The people turned to Moses for his intercession which the Lord heard. Yet, the people promptly found something else to complain about. Watching some of their fellow men and women die from the Lord's fire the survivors still failed to give thanks. Instead they complained more, this time about not having meat to eat. The manna God provided was not sufficient to satisfy their lusting hearts (Num. 11:4-9). This time, when Moses heard the people complaining, as he listened to 'the people weep throughout their families, every man in the door of his tent' Moses was displeased, as the Lord's anger was again kindled, this time 'greatly' (Num. 11:10).

Moses was exhausted by the people's continual complaining, even though all was provided to them supernaturally. This time Moses called out to God to be relieved from the burden of the people's constant complaining. The answer was provided by God as Moses was directed to choose seventy elders who received the Spirit of the Lord. Some of the Lord's Spirit was taken off Moses and placed on these men so they could share with Moses the 'burden of the people'.

The Lord then answered the cries of the people Himself by providing meat for them to eat. However, the Lord used the opportunity to further punish the complainers. So much meat was provided to the people, all 603,550 (Num. 1:46), that they could eat for a full month, eating until they actually loathed the meat (Num. 11:18-21). Not only did the people loathe the excess of meat, those same people who had lusted after the meat paid the price for their sinful complaining. While chewing the very meat they had cried out for, the 'Lord smote the people with a great plague' (Num. 11:33-34) thus purging those whose hearts sinfully lusted. This place was named

'*Kibroth-hattaavah*: because there they buried the people that lusted' (Num. 11:35). Let us remember to always give thanks for the provision provided us by God seeking always to know the will of God and always supporting our spiritual leaders given to us by God.

Let us try to learn the lessons of always coming to the Lord making 'a joyful noise' serving Him 'with gladness' and 'singing' knowing 'we are his people, and the sheep of his pasture' knowing always that the Lord's presence requires that we 'enter into his gates with thanksgiving and into his courts with praise' 'being thankful unto him, and blessing his name' 'for the Lord is good' (Ps. 100).

The Israelites failed to give thanks for the blessing of the Lord who was watching over them and protecting them and dwelling with them. Being provided manna from heaven daily the Israelites failed to give thanks and instead longed for meat and a day gone by when meat was available: 'He that regardeth the day, regardeth it unto the Lord; and he that regardeth not the day, to the Lord he doth not regard it. He that eateth, eateth to the Lord, for he giveth God thanks; and he that eateth not, to the Lord he eateth not, and giveth God thanks' (Rom. 14:6).

In essence, we must learn that the glory must always go to the Lord and the glory starts with our giving thanks and accepting His provisions. Manna came from the commanded clouds from above and the opened doors of heaven; manna was good enough for angels (Ps. 78:23-25). Importantly, for our discussion of the angels of the Lord, Psalm 78 continues to describe the wilderness lusting of the people and the wrath brought by the Lord and the wrath against the Egyptians which motivated Pharaoh to let God's people go. Scripture describes the means of God's wrath 'by sending evil angels among them' (Ps. 78:49).

The mystery of some of the ways of the Lord will only be answered when we come to the Lord after our own rest. Until then we should seek truth through Scripture: 'All scripture is given by inspiration of God, and is profitable for doctrine, for reproof, for correction, for instruction in righteousness: That the man of God may be perfect, thoroughly furnished unto all good works' (2 Tim. 3:16-17).

Snakes bring God's wrath yet symbolize His mercy

Manna is called angel food, yet it did not please Israel as they sojourned through the wilderness destroying all of Canaan and the cities of Canaan. This sojourn was as they journeyed from mount Hor (the burial place of Aaron) along the Red Sea and around the land of Edom. During this arduous trek on foot 'the people spake against God, and against Moses' they said: 'Wherefore have ye brought us up out of Egypt to die in the wilderness? for there is no bread, neither is there any water; and our soul loatheth this light bread [manna]' (Num. 21:4-5). The wrath of God fell upon the murmurers using 'fiery serpents' which bit and killed many. These venomous snakes with a burning bite could kill and not always immediately, allowing some of the people time to repent.

The repentance was brought about by the pain, death and suffering of the people. They sought Moses' intercession with the Lord as they confessed their sinful complaining. The Lord heard Moses' prayers for the people:

> And the Lord said unto Moses, Make thee a fiery serpent, and set it upon a pole: and it shall come to pass, that every one that is bitten, when he looketh upon it, shall live.
>
> And Moses made a serpent of brass, and put it upon a pole, and it come to pass, that if a serpent had bitten any man, when he beheld the serpent of brass, he lived (Num. 21:8-9).

Importantly for us today is what Jesus Christ tells us to learn from the story of the fiery serpents:

> And as Moses lifted up the serpent in the wilderness, even so must the Son of man be lifted up: That whosoever believeth in him should not perish, but have eternal life. For God sent not his Son into the world to condemn the world; but that the world through him might be saved.
>
> He that believeth on him is not condemned: but he that believeth not is condemned already, because he hath not believed in the name of the only begotten Son of God.
>
> And this is the condemnation, that light is come into the world, and men loved darkness rather than light, because their deeds

were evil. For every one that doeth evil hateth the light, neither cometh to the light, lest his deeds should be reproved. But he that doeth truth cometh to the light, that his deeds may be made manifest, that they are wrought in God (John 3:14-21).

Hornets used by God to carry out His promises

God's evil angels may take the form of small persuasive earthly creatures. In the Old Testament the Lord's fear was sent before His people into the lands to drive out various enemies, including the Hivite, Canaanite, and the Hittite peoples. To protect His people and to glorify His name God used an angel to drive these peoples out of the promised land. God sent His fear first along with hornets which slowly but surely cleared the lands of the human enemies (Exod. 23:27-29). God promised His people he would keep His covenant and swore:

If thou shalt say in thine heart, These nations are more than I; how can I dispossess them?

Thou shalt not be afraid of them: but shalt well remember what the Lord thy God did unto Pharaoh, and unto all Egypt;

The great temptations which thine eyes saw, and the signs, and the wonders, and the mighty hand, and the stretched out arm, whereby the Lord thy God brought thee out: so shall the Lord thy God do unto all the people of whom thou art afraid.

Moreover the Lord thy God will send the hornet among them, until they that are left, and hide themselves from thee, be destroyed.

Thou shalt not be affrighted at them: for the Lord thy God is among you, a mighty God and terrible.

And the Lord thy God will put out those nations before thee by little and little: thou mayest not consume them at once, lest the beasts of the field increase upon thee (Deut. 7:17-22).

Psalm 78:49 speaks of God's wrath and anger in Egypt and thereafter being carried out on His behalf by His 'evil angels'. The ways of the Lord are beyond us. If able, most generals would move quickly to strike down their enemy in one full swoop; yet, God knew that if the enemies in the promised land were met in battle and all killed, their bodies would have led to an overflow of wild animals, insects and pestilence from the invisible world of microbes. In the time of the writing of the Old Testament how could mere mortal man have known such wonders and devastations of the unseen microbiological world unless God Himself was the inspiration? Yes, the Lord promised His people: 'And I sent the hornet before you, which drove them out from before you, even the two kings of the Amorites; but not with thy sword, nor with thy bow' (Josh. 24:12). All the glory goes to God, then and now.

Psalm 44 succinctly describes this glory of the Lord and where our focus must be:

> We have heard with our ears, O God, our fathers have told us, what work thou didst in their days, in the times of old.
>
> How thou didst drive out the heathen with thy hand, and plantedst them; how thou didst afflict the people, and cast them out.
>
> For they got not the land in possession by their own sword, neither did their own arm save them: but thy right hand, and thine arm, and the light of thy countenance, because thou hadst a favour unto them.
>
> Thou art my King, O God: command deliverances for Jacob.
>
> Through thee will we push down our enemies: through thy name will we tread them under that rise up against us.
>
> For I will not trust in my bow, neither shall my sword save me.
>
> But thou hast saved us from our enemies, and hast put them to shame that hated us.
>
> In God we boast all the day long, and praise thy name for ever. Selah (Ps. 44:1-8).

In the spiritual war going on in the invisible world today, as it was in the time of Israel's rescue from Egypt, the question of were there other angels who came with the angel sent of the Lord is surely answered in the positive. 'And when we cried unto the Lord, he heard our voice, and sent an angel, and hath brought us forth out of Egypt: and, behold, we are in Kadesh, a city in the uttermost of thy border' (Num. 20:16).

Ravens provide for Elijah

The prophet Elijah, whose name means 'Yahweh is God', stirred the anger of King Ahab and his notorious queen Jezebel when Elijah told Ahab, 'As the Lord God of Israel liveth, before whom I stand, there shall not be dew nor rain these years, but according to my word' (1 Kgs. 17:1). Ahab was defiant of the commands of God and more greatly provoked 'the Lord God of Israel to anger than all the kings of Israel that were before him' (1 Kgs. 16:32, 33) when King Ahab casually and openly sinned by building an altar for the pagan god Baal of the Zidonians, Ahab's wife's people.

After the message was delivered to King Ahab the Lord told Elijah to leave Israel proper to hide from the dangers. King Ahab and Jezebel had successfully turned many of the Jews away from the Living God to worshipping the idol Baal; they would not hesitate to sin by killing God's prophet.

Just as Elijah had fled from Israel to the brook Cherith in submission to the word of God, the ravens fed the prophet Elijah in submission to the word of God. '[God] commanded the ravens to feed [Elijah] there ... and the ravens brought him bread and flesh in the morning, and bread and flesh in the evening' (1 Kgs. 17:4, 6). Later, after Elijah had completed the challenge with the priests of Baal and told King Ahab to leave in his chariot because the rain was coming the Scripture leaves the question of whether it was the holy angels of God who supernaturally carried Elijah as he ran seventeen straight miles to Jezreel from Mount Carmel beating King Ahab's chariot. Scripture says, 'And the hand of the Lord was on Elijah; and he girded up his loins, and ran before Ahab to the entrance of Jezreel' (1 Kgs. 18:46).

Bears bring swift punishment to youthful mockers
After taking up the mantle of Elijah, Elisha called upon the power of the Lord to heal the waters of Jericho which had caused death and been barren. A group of young men from Bethal mocked and cursed Elisha by challenging his prophetic office, apparently not knowing he had received a double portion of the power of the Holy Spirit which had been upon the most famous prophet Elijah (2 Kgs. 2:23-24, 9-13). Elisha responded to the forty two young men's challenges by cursing them with the immediate response of their violent death from 'two she bears' who came out of the woods upon the prophet's voice of the Lord (2 Kgs. 2:24-25).

Lions will obey God's command

Lions may be provoked or calmed by the Lord's angels. 'My God hath sent his angel, and hath shut the lions' mouths' (Dan. 6:22). In the Book of Daniel the lions were calmed and did no harm. However, Scripture also tells of when lions are used to punish those who refuse to honour God's Word or God's anointed men.

'A certain man of the sons of the prophets said unto his neighbour in the word of the Lord, Smite [strike] me, I pray thee. And the man refused to smite him. Then said he [the prophet] unto him, Because thou has not obeyed the voice of the Lord, behold, as soon as thou art departed from me, a lion shall slay thee. And as soon as he was departed from him, a lion found him, and slew him' (1 Kgs. 20:35-36). The question is asked whether the vicious acts of this lion were in fact the Word of the Lord being displayed as 'the fierceness of his anger, wrath, and indignation, and trouble, by sending evil angels among them' as described in Psalm 78:49 (referring to the various plagues, including animal/creature plagues in Egypt)?

The 'sons of the prophets' are probably the sons of the prophets who are referred to when Scripture tells us: 'For it was so, when Jezebel cut off the prophets of the Lord, that Obadiah [who feared the Lord greatly (v.3)] took an hundred prophets, and hid them by fifty in a cave, and fed them with bread and water' (1 Kgs. 18:4).

Chapter 18

Balaam and the Speaking Ass Whose Eyes Were First Opened to View God's Angel

Give freely the Word of God as it is freely given you; do not follow the unrighteous lead of Balaam.

When Jesus sent His disciples out with power against unclean spirits, to cast them out, and to heal all manner of sickness and all manner of disease, He commanded them: 'Go preach, saying, The kingdom of heaven is at hand. Heal the sick, cleanse the lepers, raise the dead, cast out devils: freely ye have received, freely give' (Matt. 10:1, 8). God's ways are clearly revealed in Scripture: 'He that spared not his own Son, but delivered him up for us all, how shall he not with him also freely give us all things?' (Rom. 8:32). Only through the Spirit of God can we know 'the things that are freely given to us of God' (1 Cor. 2:12-13).

At the end of Scripture we are again told by both 'the Spirit' and Christ Jesus: 'Come. And let him that heareth say, Come. And let him that is athirst come. And whosoever will, let him take the water of life freely' (Rev. 22:17). The Lord thy God is always willing to show mercy for those who seek His mercy through repentance: 'I will heal their backsliding, I will love them freely: for mine anger is turned away from him...The ways of the Lord are right, and the just shall walk in them: but the transgressors shall fall therein'(Hos.13:4; 14: 4, 9).

Death will surely follow if you seek the world's reward as Balaam

Scripture makes clear that even though Balaam was warned; he continued in his ways which were sinful; and, he was assured to receive 'the reward of unrighteousness' (2 Pet. 2:13).

Having eyes full of adultery, and that cannot cease from sin; beguiling unstable souls: an heart they have exercised with covetous practices; cursed children: Which have forsaken the right way, and are gone astray, following the way of Balaam the son of Bosor, who loved the wages of unrighteousness;

But was rebuked for his iniquity: the dumb ass speaking with man's voice forbad the madness of the prophet (2 Pet. 2:14-16).

Behind the cute story of the speaking ass are serious truths

The story of Balaam begins in Numbers 22 where the king of Moab, Balak, sought the hireling prophet Balaam to come and curse the people of Israel who were a great number; Balak sent his messengers 'with the rewards of divination' meaning payment for services (Num. 22:3-7). The story continues with Balaam requesting Balak's messengers to remain at his home for the evening while he speaks to God for His revelation; Balaam's request is answered: 'God came unto Balaam, and said, What men are these with thee? Balaam said unto God, Balak the son of Sippor, king of Moab, hath sent unto me, saying, Behold, there is a people come out of Egypt, which covereth the face of the earth: come now, curse me them; peradventure I shall be able to overcome them, and drive them out. And God said unto Balaam, Thou shalt not curse the people: for they are blessed' (Num. 22:8-12).

Balaam, this time, complied with God's Word by refusing to go with Balak's messengers who returned to their king. Again though, Balak sent more of his princes who brought with them for Balaam more payment for Balaam's cursing the people of Israel. The payment included promises of promotion to 'very great honour' and a promise from the king to 'do whatsoever thou sayest unto me' (Num. 22:15-17).

God's message was clearly and directly spoken to Balaam: **Do not go.** Balaam's answer to Balak's second set of messengers shows that his heart sought worldly rewards and that he would not abide by God's word: Balaam answered 'If Balak would give me his house full of silver and gold, I cannot go beyond the word of the Lord my God, to do less or more' (Num. 22:18). Here is the evil essence of the 'error' or 'doctrine' of Balaam which is spoken of throughout Scripture.

Balaam again had the men of Balak stay the night while he sought God's Word. 'And God came unto Balaam at night, and said unto him, If the men come to call thee, rise up, and go with them; but yet the word which I shall say unto thee, that shalt thou do' (Num. 22:19-20). Balaam's disobedient heart caused the Lord to become angry: 'And Balaam rose up in the morning, and saddled his ass, and went with the princes of Moab. And God's anger was kindled because he went: and the angel of the Lord stood in the way for an adversary against him. Now he was riding upon his ass, and his two servants were with him' (Num. 22:21-22). The story continues:

And the ass saw the angel of the Lord standing in the way, and his sword drawn in his hand: and the ass turned aside out of the way, and went into the field: and Balaam smote the ass, to turn her into the way.

But the angel of the Lord stood in the path of the vineyards, a wall being on this side, and a wall on that side.

And when the ass saw the angel of the Lord, she thrust herself unto the wall, and crushed Balaam's foot against the wall: and he smote her again.

And the angel of the Lord went further, and stood in a narrow place, where was no way to turn either to the right hand or to the left.

And when the ass saw the angel of the Lord, she fell down under Balaam: and Balaam's anger was kindled, and he smote the ass with a staff.

And the Lord opened the mouth of the ass, and she said unto Balaam, What have I done unto thee, that thou hast smitten me these three times?

And Balaam said unto the ass, Because thou hast mocked me: I would there were a sword in mine hand, for now would I kill thee.

And the ass said unto Balaam, Am not I thine ass, upon which thou hast ridden ever since I was thine unto this day? was I ever wont to do so unto thee? And he said, Nay.

Then the Lord opened the eyes of Balaam, and he saw the angel of the Lord standing in the way, and his sword drawn in his hand: and he bowed down his head, and fell flat on his face.

And the angel of the Lord said unto him, Wherefore hast thou smitten thine ass these times three times? behold, I went out to withstand thee, because thy way is perverse before me:

And the ass saw me, and turned from me these three times: unless she had turned from me, surely now also I had slain thee, and saved her alive.

And Balaam said unto the angel of the Lord, I have sinned; for I knew not that thou stoodest in the way against me: now therefore, if it displease thee, I will get me back again.

And the angel of the Lord said unto Balaam, Go with the men: but only the word that I shall speak unto thee, that thou shalt speak. So Balaam went with the princes of Balak (Num. 22:23-35).

Though Balaam fell down and said he only knew of God's displeasure because of the sight of the Lord's angel, the Scripture makes clear Balaam's heart was not in agreement with the ways God had spoken to him and instead Balaam was rebelling in his heart against God, seeking worldly rewards of gold, silver and esteem instead of revering God's Word. Balaam later does honour God by refusing to curse Israel and on each occasion gives a blessing to the people of Israel, which apparently caused Balaam's heart to grieve due to his loss of worldly rewards (Num. 23:7-10; 23:18-24; 24:3-9; Josh. 24:9-10).

Prefaced by the words, 'Thus saith the Lord God of Israel', Joshua makes clear that Balaam's heart was desiring to curse Israel, noting that:

> Then Balak the son of Zippor, king of Moab, arose and warred against Israel, and sent and called Balaam the son of Beor to curse you: *But I would not hearken unto Balaam; therefore he blessed you still: so I delivered you out of his hand.* [The Israelites thereafter crossed the Jordan and came into Jericho] (Josh. 24:9-10; see Deuteronomy 23:4-5).

Balaam was promised great wealth if he would curse the chosen people of Israel. But the Lord 'would not hearken unto Balaam'.

The reward of this world is despised by the Spirit of God. 'Woe unto them! for they have gone in the way of Cain, and ran greedily after the error of Balaam for reward, and perished in the gainsaying of Core' (Jude 11). Here Balaam's sin is compared to Cain and Core (Korah): we find the sin of 'Cain who was of that wicked one' and slew his righteous brother (1 John 3:12) and who rejected God's provision for acceptance with Himself (Gen. 4:1-12); and, the sin of Korah (Core) was rebellion against duly constituted authority (Num. 16:1-3).

Thus, the story of Balaam and his ass warns us against some serious pitfalls for ministers and all of us who look to the world for reward instead of God. 'The error of Balaam' was that he hired himself out as a prophet and epitomizes deceit and covetousness (cf. Num. 22-24; 2 Pet. 2:15; Rev. 2:14). Jesus also teaches 'the error of Balaam' as He speaks to 'the angel of the church in Pergamos' by explaining further: 'the doctrine of Balaam, who taught Balak to cast a stumblingblock before the children of Israel, to eat things sacrificed unto idols, and to commit fornication'; Jesus continues by warning them to: 'Repent: or else I will come unto thee quickly, and will fight against them with the sword of my mouth' (Rev. 2:12, 14-16).

Physical and spiritual death is the punishment of selling yourself out for hired religious work. Balaam was slain by the sword of Israel when Moses followed the command of the Lord to avenge the children of Israel by making war against the Midianites (Num. 31:1-8).

Let us be forewarned to honour the direction and commands of the Word of God which admonishes us to seek the spiritual kingdom of God and His righteousness. The Lord God warns us to turn away and run from the worldly rewards, gold and silver which last only until our sure death. Instead we should always seek God's face and His rewards. It seems all too often our fellow man forgets these teachings that Jesus could not have made any clearer:

> For what is a man profited, if he shall gain the whole world, and lose his own soul? or what shall a man give in exchange for his soul? (Matt. 16:26).

Knowing full well God's desire for our lives let us not be caught in the hypocrisy of 'Balaam when he said unto the angel of the Lord, I have sinned; for I knew not that thou stoodest in the way against me:

now therefore, if it displease thee, I will get me back again.' Balaam knew all too well, as we know, the will of our Lord; and, if we, as Balaam, sin we will be judged. Remember, Jesus promised: 'For the Son of man shall come in the glory of his Father with his angels: and then he shall reward every man according to his works' (Matt. 16:27).

Chapter 19

Angels Called to Minister For and To Jesus Christ

Anyone who downplays the comforting power of angels is not basing that conclusion upon Scripture. Jesus called upon angels on many occasions to proclaim His arrival, His glory, or strengthen Him, care for Him, and comfort Him during His earthly ministry. The fact that Jesus, who was God Incarnate, called angels to His side in times of need is telling.

Joseph and Mary see and communicate with angels
The angel of the Lord appeared to Joseph in a dream, telling him the baby in Mary's womb is the Saviour:

> Thou son of David, fear not to take unto thee Mary thy wife: for that which is conceived in her is of the Holy Ghost.
> And she shall bring forth a son, and thou shalt call his name JESUS: for he shall save his people from their sins.
> Now all this was done, that it might be fulfilled which was spoken of the Lord by the prophet, saying,
> Behold, a virgin shall be with child, and shall bring forth a son, and they shall call his name Emmanuel, which being interpreted is, God with us.
> Then Joseph being raised from sleep did as the angel of the Lord had bidden him, and took unto him his wife (Matt. 1:20-24).

The angel Gabriel appeared to Mary with the blessed news of Jesus' forthcoming birth (Luke 1:26-28; see Isaiah 7:14). As already described, the shepherds were graced with the appearance of an angel announcing the Messiah's birth (Luke 2:9-10); and, then with the angel there appeared a multitude of the heavenly host praising God (Luke 2:13-14).

Angels protect baby Jesus by warning Joseph of danger

Jesus and His parents were protected and provided for while He was just a babe. Joseph was told to go with his family immediately to Egypt to escape the coming assault by Herod who would try to kill the Christ (Matt. 2:13-18). While in Egypt Joseph was again visited by an angel who told him to return to Israel since the threat was gone; Herod was dead (Matt. 2:20). The gifts from the 'wise men from the east' surely paid all of the costs in order to make the trips to and from Egypt. The valuable gifts enabled Jesus and His family to comfortably make the long trips:

> There came wise men from the east to Jerusalem, Saying,
> Where is he that is born King of the Jews? for we have seen his star in the east, and are come to worship him (Matt. 2:1-2).
> They departed; and, lo, the star, which they saw in the east, went before them, till it came and stood over where the young child was.
> When they saw the star, they rejoiced with exceeding great joy (Matt. 2:9-10).

After worshipping and giving their gifts of gold, frankincense and myrrh, the wise men were 'warned of God in a dream that they should not return to Herod' (Matt. 2:11-12).

Scripture foretells of the Messiah born in Bethlehem

Some questions arise as to how these wise men knew the meaning of the star in the sky. They must have searched and studied the Scriptures, praying for and receiving understanding, based upon the Books of Genesis and Numbers and the prophets Isaiah and Micah:

> Judah, thou art he whom thy brethren shall praise: thy hand shall be in the neck of thine enemies; thy father's children shall bow down before thee...
> The sceptre shall not depart from Judah, nor a lawgiver from between his feet, until Shiloh come; and unto him shall the gathering of the people be (Gen. 49:8, 10).

I shall see him, but not now: I shall behold him, but not nigh: *there shall come a Star out of Jacob, and a Sceptre shall rise out of Israel,* and shall smite the corners of Moab, and destroy all the children of Sheth (Num. 24:17).

Arise, shine; for thy light is come, and the glory of the Lord is risen upon thee.

For, behold, the darkness shall cover the earth, and gross darkness the people: *but the Lord shall arise upon thee, and his glory shall be seen upon thee.*

And the Gentiles shall come to thy light, and kings to the brightness of thy rising (Is. 60:1-3).

But thou, Bethlehem Ephratah, though thou be little among the thousands of Judah, yet out of thee shall he come forth unto me that is to be ruler in Israel; whose goings forth have been from of old, from everlasting (Mic. 5:2).

God's ways are surely not man's ways as it was Gentile wise men who came to understand and respond to these Scriptures including Isaiah's and Micah's prophecy and not any of the Jewish wise men. Possibly, God sent an angel to these wise men of the east to enlighten their understanding of Scripture concerning the coming Messiah.

Angels strengthen and comfort Jesus

Angels came to Jesus to comfort and strengthen Him during some of His weakest moments, both physically and emotionally. Remember, Jesus who came 'in the likeness of sinful flesh, and for sin, condemned sin in the flesh' (Rom. 8:3). After the three temptations by the devil, called 'the tempter', were spurned by Jesus, speaking the Word of God, all after spending forty long days and nights of fasting in the wilderness, angels came; He was comforted and cared for by angels (Matt. 4:2, 11).

In the Garden of Gethsemane Jesus was strengthened and comforted by angels after He had prayed to honour His Father's will and not His own. Jesus made this prayer although He knew the following day He would suffer brutally and then be crucified, and

His Father would turn away His face, leaving His only begotten Son separated from the Father for the first time.

The Gospel of Luke focuses these earnest moments in time with trembling clarity, dispelling any question about the real severity of the punishment Jesus accepted and received to condemn sin in His flesh (Rom. 8:3) for the world:

> And he was withdrawn from them about a stone's cast, and kneeled down, and prayed,
> Saying, 'Father, if thou be willing, remove this cup from me: nevertheless not my will, but thine, be done.'
> And there appeared an angel unto him from heaven, strengthening him.
> And being in an agony he prayed more earnestly: and his sweat was as it were great drops of blood falling down to the ground (Luke 22:41-44).

Proclaim, Christ is risen! Proclaim, Christ is risen!

An angel of supreme strength rolled away the stone at the entrance to Jesus' tomb before announcing Jesus' resurrection.

> As it began to dawn toward the first day of the week, came Mary Magdalene and the other Mary to see the sepulchre.
> And, behold, there was a great earthquake: for the angel of the Lord descended from heaven, and came and rolled back the stone from the door, and sat upon it. His countenance was like lightening, and his raiment white as snow:
> And for fear of him the keepers did shake, and became as dead men.
> *And the angel answered and said unto the women, Fear not ye: for I know that ye seek Jesus, which was crucified. He is not here: for he is risen, as he said. Come, see the place where the Lord lay* (Matt. 28:1-6).

The angel(s) involved in the proclamation of the Risen Christ at the grave are described in the Gospels as: 'His countenance was like lightening, and his raiment white as snow' (Matt. 28:3); 'They saw a young man sitting ... clothed in a long white garment' (Mark 16:5); 'two men stood by them in shining garments' (Luke 24:2-7); 'And

Mary seeth two angels in white sitting' (John 20:12). Surely, these angels were smiling as they brought this most wonderful message of death being defeated, promised from the foundations of time.

Christ's ascension

Just before Jesus physically departed from earth He promised His disciples 'ye shall receive power, after that the Holy Ghost is come upon you: and ye shall be witnesses unto me both in Jerusalem, and in all Judaea, and in Samaria, and unto the uttermost part of the earth' (Acts 1:8). *Never forget this command from Jesus to be witnesses for the Risen Christ to the uttermost parts of the earth and 'preach the Gospel to every creature'* (Mark 16:15).

When Jesus left His apostles the final time 'while they beheld, he was taken up; and a cloud received him out of their sight. And while they looked stedfastly toward heaven as he went up, behold, two men stood by them in white apparel; Which also said, Ye men of Galilee, why stand ye gazing up into heaven? this same Jesus, which is taken up from you into heaven, shall so come in like manner as ye have seen him go into heaven' (Acts 1:9-11).

Let us always be waiting and anxiously looking to the sky for His promised return. Scripture tells of our blessing if found watching for His return (Luke 12:37, 38, 40). 'In his sight ... all things are naked and opened unto the eyes of him with whom we have to do' (Heb. 4:13). 'For the word of God is quick, and powerful, and sharper than any two-edged sword, piercing even to the dividing asunder of soul and spirit, and of the joints and marrow, and is a discerner of the thoughts and intents of the heart' (Heb. 4:12). I trust the Word when it speaks to my heart: 'There remaineth therefore a rest to the people of God' (Heb. 4:8). 'Watch therefore for ye know not what hour your Lord doth come' (Matt. 24:42).

Jesus' physical and visible return

When Jesus returns visibly and physically to this earth in His glory a vast host of angelic beings will accompany Him: *'With his mighty angels, In flaming fire taking vengeance on them that know not God, and that obey not the gospel of our Lord Jesus Christ:* Who shall be punished with everlasting destruction from the presence of the Lord, and from the glory of his power' (2 Thess. 1:7-9; Matt. 16:27; 25:31). And, as they have done since their creation by Jesus Himself, angels will worship and exalt Him for all of eternity (Rev. 5:11-14).

Chapter 20

Let There be Light

I pray for all who read this that God, through the power of His Son and Holy Spirit, shall command for you: 'Let there be light' (Gen. 1:3). The question is, will you bow now (Eph. 3:14) believing in faith that Christ Jesus was made sin for us by His death on the cross as a perfect sacrifice to the Father? (2 Cor. 5:21). Or, will you wait to bow later in ultimate judgment and humble submission (Is. 45:23; Rom. 14:10-12), and then to be cast for eternity into the lake of fire prepared for the devil and his angels? (Rev. 20:15; Matt. 25:41, 46).

Holy Scripture is clear: 'Jesus as a man ... humbled himself, and became obedient unto death, even the death of the cross. Wherefore God also hath highly exalted him, and given him a name which is above every name: That at the name of Jesus every knee should bow, of things in heaven, and things in earth, and things under the earth; And that every tongue should confess that Jesus Christ is Lord, to the glory of God the Father' (Phil. 2:8-11). And, that: 'Neither is there salvation in any other: for there is none other name under heaven given among men, whereby we must be saved' (Acts 4:12).

In spite of the clear teaching of the Word of God, Satan, that evil and malignant being that he is, goes on his desperate and hopeless way of trying to defeat the plans of God. Satan began his deceitful effort to defeat the plans of God when the serpent, embodied by Lucifer, in the Garden questioned Eve about God's Word by misstating it, leading her to eat the forbidden fruit (Gen. 3:1-13). The command of God is instantly fulfilled when He, the Holy Spirit, says to some hearts, 'Let there be light!' Thus the entrance of His Word gives light (Ps. 119:130). Those to whom He speaks are immediately delivered from the power of darkness, and are translated into the kingdom of His dear Son Jesus the Christ (Col. 1:13). Trust in the Word of God when it tells us that 'every knee shall bow' to Jesus (Phil. 2:10).

Romans 10:13 and 14 tells us that whosoever calls upon the name of the Lord will be saved; pray for the faith to make your call into the light. Jesus promises us that if we believe in Him and repent: 'I stand at the door, and knock: if any man hear my voice, and open the door, I will come in to him, and will sup with him, and he with me. To him that overcometh will I grant to sit with me in my throne, even as I also overcame, and am set down with my Father in his throne' (Rev. 3:20-21).

Faith will allow you to bow in glorious praise as an heir of God being assured of enjoying all of His promises of glory: 'And the glory which thou [God the Father] gavest me I have given them; that they may be one, even as we are one: I in them, and thou in me, that they may be made perfect in one ... that the love wherewith thou hast loved me may be in them, and I in them' (John 17:23, 26). The light of God's eternal love dwelling within you is available if only you will ask.

PART 2

Chapter 21

The Truth about Satan and Demons According to God's Word

Three Foundational Definitions

Fallen Angels: Scripture teaches that Satan and the fallen angels (demons) were created sinless and later fell (Is. 14:12-15; Rev. 12:3-4). Some of the number of angels 'did not keep their own domain' but fell under divine displeasure, beings reserved 'for judgment of the great day' (Jude 6). Many Bible teachers believe that these imprisoned fallen angels include the angels that cohabitated with mortal women as described in Genesis 6:1-2; the fallen angels' imprisonment is a special punishment for their attempt to pollute the lineage of the seed of the woman which Satan knew would lead to him eating dust by the birth of Jesus as Messiah.

Demons: (Gk. *daimon*, and its derivative *daimonion*). Used once in the NT (Acts 17:18, NIV, 'foreign gods'; NASB, 'deities,') for deity, but usually referring to the ministers of the devil (Luke 4:35; 9:1, 42; John 10:21; etc.). Satan is called the 'ruler of the demons' (Matt. 9:34; 12:24; Mark 3:22; Luke 11:15; Gk. *archon ton daimonion*). Demons are inferior spirit beings, Satan's angels who 'did not keep their own domain' (Jude 6; Matt. 25:41; Rev. 12:7, 9).

Demoniac: (Gk. *daimonizomai*, 'to be under the power of a demon' rendered 'demon possessed' or 'demoniac'). A term frequently used in the NT of one under the influence of a demon. The verb 'to be demonized' occurs, in one form or another, seven times in Matthew, four times in Mark, once in Luke and once in John.

Chapter 22

Demons Were Real to Jesus

Only by denying the very actions and words of Jesus could anyone deny the reality of demons and their possession of men. Were the actions and words of Jesus concerning demons, evil spirits and the devil just a pretence and show on His part, whereas His other actions and words were not?

On repeated occasions Scripture explains how Jesus treated cases of demonic possession as realities. Jesus speaks to and directs the demons in men by 'rebuking', 'commanding', and 'casting out' the unclean spirits. Jesus speaks directly to the evil spirits as well: Jesus addressed the demons who identified themselves as 'Legion', commanding them to leave, responding to their pleading not to be punished before their time, and finally granting them permission to enter a nearby herd of swine (Matt. 8:28-32; Mark 5:8-12). Jesus also directly addressed the unclean spirit: 'Be quiet, and come out of him!' (Mark 1:25; Luke 4:35).

Jesus made clear His relationship with Jehovah God through His actions of casting out demons. He deliberately argued with the Jews on the assumption of the reality of demonic possession, affirming that His casting out demons by the Spirit of God proved that the kingdom of God had come to them (Matt. 12:23-28; Luke 11:14-26).

When Jesus' disciples were unable to cast out a demon and questioned Him, Jesus revealed that: 'This kind cannot come out by anything but prayer and fasting' (Mark 9:29). In the holy and solemn act of calling and appointing the apostles: 'He appointed twelve, that they might be with Him, and that He might send them out to preach, and to have authority to cast out the demons.' When the seventy disciples returned with joy, and with perhaps some pride, they said to

Him: 'Lord, even the demons are subject to us in Your name' (Luke 10:17).

Demons can cause illness

Scriptural evidence points to actual possession by spirits. 'The demonized were incapable of separating their own consciousness and ideas from the influence of the demon, their own identity being merged, and to that extent lost, in that of their tormentors. In this respect the demonized state was also kindred to madness' (Ederscheim, *Life of Jesus*, 1:608).

The Gospels constantly distinguish between demonic possession and all forms of mere disease, although sometimes they occurred together. 'When the sun did set, they brought unto him all that were diseased, and them that were possessed with devils. And he healed many that were sick of divers diseases, and cast out many devils; and suffered not the devils to speak, because they knew him' (Mark 1:32; 34). 'Behold, they brought to him a dumb man possessed with a devil. And when the devil was cast out, the dumb spake' (Matt. 9:32-33).

> And his fame went throughout all Syria: and they brought unto him all sick people that were taken with divers diseases and torments, and those which were possessed with devils, and those which were lunatick, and those that had the palsy; and he healed them (Matt. 4:24).

Some people may conclude demoniacs (persons whose bodies demons had entered) are always afflicted with especially severe diseases, either bodily or mental, such as depression, melancholy, insanity, paralysis, blindness, deafness, loss of speech, epilepsy, etc. However, Scripture distinguishes between the disease and the possession. When Jesus called His disciples to Him 'he gave them power against unclean spirits, to cast them out, and to heal all manner of sickness and all manner of disease' (Matt. 10:1; see Mark 3:15; Luke 9:1). In Mark 6:13 the disciples 'cast out many devils, and anointed with oil many that were sick, and healed them' (see Luke 6:17-18).

The Bible constantly teaches that the actions and utterances in demonic possessions were those of the evil spirits. The demons are the actual agents in the cases. There are many statements indicating this: 'The unclean spirits, when they saw him, fell down before him, and cried, saying, Thou are the Son of God' (Mark 3:11); 'So the devils besought Him, saying ...' (Matt. 8:31); 'and when the unclean spirit had torn him [throwing him into convulsions], and cried out with a loud voice, and he came out of him' (Mark 1:26; see Luke 4:35). Similar stories of demons are found in Mark 9:20-26; Luke 8:2; 9:42; and, Acts 5:16.

Some of the facts recorded about demoniacs are not compatible with any theory of mere bodily or mental disease. A good example of such demon possession is given in three Gospels where the demons asked and received from Christ permission to pass from the demoniac into the herd of swine (Matt. 8; Mark 5; Luke 8).

Jesus I know and Paul I know – but who are you?
Obviously, persons with various disease like epilepsy, lunacy or insanity do not go around making claims of people's holiness. There may have been a sort of double consciousness indicated in some of these cases. At times, even though the man is demon possessed, the spoken words appear to come from the man and not the evil spirit. Scripture makes a distinction between 'the man, in whom was the evil spirit' and 'the evil spirit' who leaped on the sons of Sceva and overcame them (Acts 19:13-17).

The book of Acts describes a most remarkable story in which a demon retaliates by overcoming and punishing men who, without proper authority, called upon the name of Jesus without Jesus' permission. At the time of these events, magicians thought that by calling upon the name of a deity they could call upon the power of that deity. Acts 19:11-18 describes how only those totally devoted to Jesus can safely call on His name for demonic exorcism.

The story of the sons of Sceva begins with the proclamation that 'God wrought special miracles by the hands of Paul' by his laying hands upon aprons and handkerchiefs which when returned to the sick and demon possessed caused the diseases to depart and the evil spirits to go out of them. The errors of the sons of Sceva imply that they were impressed by the power of the Jesus in whose name Paul had done these miracles:

> Then certain of the vagabond Jews, exorcists, took upon them to call over them which had evil spirits the name of the Lord Jesus saying, We adjure you by Jesus who Paul preacheth. And there were seven sons of one Sceva, a Jew, and chief of the priests, which did so.
>
> And the evil spirit answered and said, Jesus I know, and Paul I know but who are ye?
>
> And the man in whom the evil spirit was leaped on them, and overcame them, and prevailed against them, so that they fled out of that house naked and wounded.
>
> And this was known to all the Jews and Greeks also dwelling at Ephesus; and fear fell on them all, and the name of the Lord Jesus was magnified (Acts 19:13-17).

Even the demons proclaimed Christ the Holy One of God

Again, there is the habitual assertion of Christ's divinity by this 'legion' of spirits and our Lord's recognition of the fact, while as yet not only the people but also the disciples did not know who He was. 'I know thee who thou art, the Holy One of God' (Mark 1:24; Luke 4:34). 'What have we to do with thee Jesus, thou Son of God?' (Matt. 8:29). 'And unclean spirits, when they saw him, fell down before him, and cried, saying, Thou art the Son of God' (Mark 3:11). 'And devils also came out of many, crying out, and saying, Thou art Christ the Son of God' (Luke 4:41).

At several places in Scripture Jesus acknowledges the demons' claims of His holiness. 'Jesus suffered not the devils to speak, because they knew him' (Mark 1:34). 'And he straitly charged them that they should not make him known' (Mark 3:12). 'And Jesus rebuking them suffered them not to speak: for they knew that he was Christ' (Luke 4:41).

Setting free those possessed by demons

Demoniacs are always set free in the New Testament. The freedom came from the word of power Jesus spoke or He entrusted to His disciples. The demons always obeyed, submitting to the power of the Christ, God's anointed one. Special religious formulas or magical exorcisms are not described in Scripture. The Word of God truly has power when properly used under the authority of Jesus.

Casting demons out is of no lasting avail unless the person possessed receives Jesus as their personal Saviour. A displaced demon will surely return and bring reinforcements: As Jesus explains:

> When the unclean spirit is gone out of a man, he walketh through dry places, seeking rest, and findeth none.
> *Then he saith, I will return into my house from whence I came out; and when he is come, he findeth it empty, swept, and garnished.*
> *Then goeth he, and taketh with himself seven other spirits more wicked than himself, and they enter in and dwell there: and the last state of that man is worse than the first.* Even so shall it be also unto this wicked generation (Matt. 12:43-45).

An 'unclean spirit' is equal to a demon. Self-reformation, without spiritual conversion, can lead to even more serious ramifications. Notice that some demons are more wicked than others, and they can repossess a person from whom they have been cast out bringing, at least in this case, seven other 'more wicked' demons.

Some demons require prayer and fasting before they will flee

To cast out certain powerful demons require special measures of faith and purification of fasting by the person calling on the demon to be gone, Jesus taught (Matt. 17:20).

The faith of the disciples was weak, even though they walked with, spoke with and lived with Jesus Christ. St. Matthew makes clear the disappointing level of faith of his company, even for the disciples who had been given such miraculous powers of healing and casting out demons. From the multitude a man cried out to Jesus for mercy on the man's son; the man's son was totally overcome by a 'devil' spirit who caused the boy to be a 'lunatick, and sore vexed: for ofttimes he falleth into the fire, and oft into the water' (Matt. 17:14-15). Jesus was upset when the man told Him His disciples had not been able to cure the boy. Understanding that Jesus could read the hearts and minds of everyone around Him, His words become more clear as Jesus answered:

O faithless and perverse generation, how long shall I be with you? how long shall I suffer you? bring him hither to me (Matt. 17:17).

The exact words Jesus used as He 'rebuked the devil' are not given, as they are not what is important for us to learn. The disciples were confused why this demon spirit had been able to resist when all the other infesting evil spirits had fled. Jesus provides an answer which indicates that some demon spirits are more powerful than others, and that the person calling upon the authority of Jesus must make physical as well as spiritual preparation. Jesus tells the disciples:

> *Because of your unbelief: for verily I say unto you, If ye have faith as a grain of mustard seed, ye shall say unto this mountain, Remove hence to yonder place; and it shall remove; and nothing shall be impossible unto you. Howbeit this kind goeth not out but by prayer and fasting* (Matt. 17:20).

Prayer combined with fasting has some peculiar power. Distrusting the power of calling upon Jesus leads to the unbelief the disciples had. The deeply spiritual calling to God for His help by prayer combined with denying the body of food can foster unique results from God.

Prayer and fasting will not always get desired results

King David repented by praying face-down in the dirt and fasting for seven days when he desired the greatest favour and forgiveness from the Lord (2 Sam. 13). God was exceedingly displeased because David had 'despised the commandment of the Lord, to do evil in [God's] sight' (2 Sam. 13:9). David's rebellion against the law began when he saw from his roof a 'very beautiful' woman bathing; David lusted after Bathsheba who was the wife of another; David's lust led to adultery which led to murder.

Bathsheba was then married to Uriah the Hittite whom David eventually had murdered (2 Sam. 11-12). *'The thing that David had done displeased the Lord' because of David's evil sins but also 'because by this deed thou hast given great occasion to the enemies of the Lord to blaspheme'* (2 Sam. 11:27; 12:14). Adultery and murder were death penalty sins but David's sin seems even more egregious considering that Uriah's name means 'Yahweh is my light'.

When David was told of his punishment from God he had already married Bathsheba who had bore him a son. David repented when he 'said unto Nathan, I have sinned against the Lord. And Nathan said unto David, The Lord also hath put away thy sin; thou shalt not die. ... The child also that is born unto thee shall surely die' (2 Sam. 12:13-14).

Nathan the prophet had spoken to King David for God; David's son from his wife Bathsheba was to die while David was allowed to live. King David's truly heartfelt repentance before God saved David's life but nothing David did thereafter could stop God's wrath. Seven days after David laid face-first in the dirt praying and fasting beseeching God for the child's life the child died (2 Sam. 12:17-18). When told of his son's death David goes to God Himself:

> Then David arose from the earth, and washed, and anointed himself, and changed his apparel, and came into the house of the Lord, and worshipped: then he came to his own house; and when he required, they set bread before him, and he did eat.
>
> Then said his servants unto him, What thing is this that thou hast done? thou didst fast and weep for the child, while it was alive; but when the child was dead, thou didst rise and eat bread.
>
> And he said, While the child was yet alive, I fasted and wept: for I said, Who can tell whether God will be gracious to me, that the child may live? But now he is dead, wherefore should I fast? can I bring him back again? I shall go to him, but he shall not return to me (2 Sam. 12:20-23).

Honouring God and respecting His decisions in times of deep sorrow and loss is possibly what made David 'a man after His own heart' (1 Sam. 13:14; Acts 13:22). When David was fasting he was humbling his soul before God (Ps. 35:13). Just as with David, whether our prayers are answered as we ask is not as important as our deep heartfelt and complete trust that whatever the answer is it is God's answer. God's ways always honour His name and His will, as we should by our honouring, respecting and worshipping our Lord. Scripture teaches that 'no good thing will [God] withhold from them that walk uprightly', seeking and striving for righteousness and obedience, and blessed is the man that trusteth in the Lord of hosts (Ps. 84:11-12).

Faith in the promise that our prayers will be answered and the sanctifying purification of our bodies by fasting while seeking spiritual power from God can give us the needed extra power over demon spirits which haunt our lives or the lives of those we love.

Other Uses of Fasting

Jesus spoke about fasting by His disciples. When asked by the scribes and Pharisees why they did not fast as other religious men did Jesus answered: 'Can the children of the bride-chamber fast, while the bridegroom is with them? as long as they have the bridegroom with them, they cannot fast. But the days will come, when the bridegroom shall be taken away from them, and then shall they fast in those days' (Mark 2:18-22; see also Matthew 9:14-17; Luke 5:33-39). The message seems to be that the disciples' joy of having the 'bridegroom', God Himself, physically with them was incompatible with the fasting; whereas, after Jesus returned to the Father in heaven, 'when the bridegroom shall be taken away from them', then it would be appropriate for the disciples to mourn His departure while at the same time seeking bodily purification and Spiritual power by fasting.

The Holy Ghost acting through Paul demonstrated the wrath which can come against those evil spirits who attempt to interfere with the preaching of and redemptive power of the Gospel of Jesus Christ. The story begins in the church in Antioch with certain prophets and teachers, including Barnabas, Simeon, Lucius of Cyrene, Manaen, and Saul known as Paul. 'As they ministered to the Lord, and fasted, the Holy Ghost said, Separate me Barnabas and Saul for the work whereunto I have called them. So they, being sent forth by the Holy Ghost, departed ...' (Acts 13:1-4). Early in their trip while travelling on the Isle of Cyprus to the city of Paphos, Paul and Barnabas were called to preach the Word of God to 'the deputy of the country, Sergius Paulus, a prudent man' (Acts 13:6-7).

Keeping company with Deputy Paulus was 'a certain sorcerer, a false prophet, a Jew, whose name was Bar-Jesus' and also known as 'Elymas the sorcerer' (Acts 13:8, 7). Elymas the sorcerer attempted to interfere with God's Word by urging the Deputy not to listen to what Paul and Barnabas said:

> Then Saul [Paul] filled with the Holy Ghost, set his eyes on him, [glared intently at the Sorcerer], And said, O full of all subtilty and all mischief, thou child of the devil, thou enemy of all righteousness, wilt thou not cease to pervert the right ways of the Lord?
>
> And now, behold, the hand of the Lord is upon thee, and thou shalt be blind, not seeing the sun for a season. And immediately there fell on him a mist and a darkness; and he went about seeking some to lead him by the hand.
>
> Then the deputy, when he saw what was done, believed, being astonished at the doctrine of the Lord (Acts 13:9-12).

The Holy Spirit through His Scripture tells us that Paul was prepared to be sent on his first missionary journey only after he and the other Christian followers prayed and fasted. Only then Paul was directed by the Word of the Holy Spirit to go. Also, this 'child of the devil', the sorcerer, was blinded, at least in part, by the extra power wrought by the prayer and fasting.

Chapter 23

Lucifer's Created Glory

Lucifer the powerful traitor to God

Lucifer sought total self-exaltation amounting to the most blasphemous heartfelt words imaginable from God's most beautifully created being. Lucifer's treachery was deserving of the ultimate eternal punishment. He was created to have supreme wisdom, beauty, and to be the ultimate consummation of perfection until he was found containing iniquity by God (Ezek. 28:15). God set him as 'the anointed cherub that covereth ... upon the holy mountain of God ... [walking] in the midst of the stones of fire' (Ezek. 28:14). Lucifer looked to wisdom by looking to within himself in all the glorious apparel he was: made of the most beautiful and valued stones, gems and jewels of earth, but forgetting the warning in Job 28 that wisdom and understanding will never be found from things of this world (Job 28:12-20). God makes clear: 'Behold, the fear of the Lord, that is wisdom; and to depart from evil is understanding' (Job 28:28).

Lucifer's name means literally 'the bright one'. The Lord God first describes his original wisdom and beauty as the ultimate consummation of perfection:

> Thou sealest up the sum, full of wisdom, and perfect in beauty.
> Thou hast been in Eden the garden of God; every precious stone was thy covering, the sardinus [deep red], topaz [yellow-green], and the diamond [brilliant light reflecting clearness], the beryl [blue green or turquoise], the onyx [bands of black, bands of transparent white and bands of dark red], and the jasper [translucent rich sky-blue or green or rosy or mingled opaline hues], the sapphire [darkly rich blue], the emerald [green or turquoise or deep fiery red], and the carbuncle [crystal emerald],

and gold: the workmanship of thy tabrets and of thy pipes was prepared in thee in the day that thou wast created.

Thou art the anointed cherub that covereth; and I have set thee so: thou was upon the holy mountain of God; thou hast walked up and down in the midst of the stones of fire.

Thou wast perfect in thy ways from the day that thou wast created, till iniquity was found in thee (Ezek. 28:12-15).

Lucifer, even though capable of appearing in the likeness of a man (Ezek. 1:5), was truly an exalted created being of God's design, making his betrayal especially notorious and dishonourable and disloyal. Consider that as a cherubim Lucifer was of an order of angels charged with guarding the holiness of God (cherubims guarded the way to the tree of life in Eden – Gen. 3:24) and two cherubims' representations were fastened with wings stretched forth on high, covering the Mercy Seat of the ark (Exod. 25:18-22). The Lord God then describes Lucifer's fall of sin after iniquity was found in his heart; his rebellious heart being described as 'the midst of thee with violence'. God's judgment follows:

I will cast thee as profane out of the mountain of God: and I will destroy thee, O covering cherub, from the midst of the stones of fire.

Thine heart was lifted up because of thy beauty, thou hast corrupted thy wisdom by reason of thy brightness: I will cast thee to the ground, I will lay thee before kings, that they may behold thee.

Thou hast defiled thy sanctuaries by the multitude of thine iniquities, by the iniquity of thy traffick; therefore will I bring forth a fire from the midst of thee, it shall devour thee, and I will bring thee to ashes upon the earth in the sight of all them that behold thee.

All they that know thee among the people shall be astonished at thee: thou shalt be a terror, and never shalt thou be any more (Ezek. 28:16-19).

For Satan's wicked rebellion he is cast down into hell as part of God's punishment; and, to emphasize God's total control and glory,

God actually raises hell to meet Satan who is speeding down faster than the speed of light towards his pit of torment (Is. 14:9). As further description of what awaits the devil and those who follow his ways Isaiah 14:15-16 continues: 'Yet thou shall be brought down to hell, to the sides of the pit. They that see thee shall narrowly look upon thee, and consider thee, saying, Is this the man that made the earth to tremble, that did shake kingdoms?'

Be forewarned about following after iniquity and hardening your heart against the ways of the Lord. Do not listen to the lies of Satan who knows his fate already. Or, your fate will be as it shall be for every child of the devil: 'Prepare slaughter for his children' (Is. 14:21). Do not forget that Jesus most clearly explained that, 'He that is not with me is against me' (Matt. 12:30).

Isaiah continues the discussion of Lucifer's punishment of being cast into hell by comparing God's righteous judgment of the King of Babylon. This king and other leaders of the nations of the world God allowed to have some earthly glory which they used wickedly against God's plan, here against the chosen nation of Israel. Clearly the designs of Lucifer are to exalt himself above God, have all others in heaven and earth worship him, and to become the independently supreme being, and completely sovereign (Is. 14:13-14).

The devil has been in the past, and is still, behind the evil enemies of Israel, as well as all enemies of God's chosen peoples and present day saints. Isaiah 14:4-6 compares Satan with how the king of Babylon's oppression of the nation of Israel ceased, as well as the cessation of the 'golden city' of Babylon, because God's wrath fell upon them sending them to hell, by describing God's wrath to fall (and hell to rise) against Satan:

> Hell from beneath is moved for thee to meet thee at thy coming: it stirreth up the dead for thee, even all the chief ones of the earth; it hath raised up from their thrones all the kings of the nations.
> All they shall speak and say unto thee, Art thou also become weak as we? art thou become like unto us?
> Thy pomp is brought down to the grave, and the noise of thy viols: the worm is spread under thee, and the worms cover thee (Is. 14:9-11).

Satan was cast out of the third heaven by God. Satan's rebellion resulted from his heart being so full of pride. Isaiah 14:12 describes Satan as: 'How art thou fallen from heaven, O Lucifer, son of the morning! how art thou cut down to the ground, which didst weaken the nations!'

Chapter 24

Satan's Five 'I wills'

Before Lucifer 'weakened' the nations he sinned mightily against his Maker by speaking these words in his heart:

> I will ascend into heaven, I will exalt my throne above the stars of God: I will sit also upon the mount of the congregation, in the sides of the north:
> I will ascend above the heights of the clouds; I will be like the most High (Is. 14:13-14).

Each of Satan's five phrases beginning with 'I will' enumerate while particularizing the extent of his sin. Lucifer's defiant imaginations are progressive cries for more and more power, culminating with absolute sovereignty by displacing the Most High God from His very throne of the entire universe. Lucifer starts with his desire to 'ascend into heaven'.

Satan's 'I will ascend into heaven'
Lucifer began by aspiring to 'ascend into heaven' and announcing his overall plan of extending his power beyond the earth as limited by God. The Scriptures not only identifies him as 'the prince of this world', 'the prince of the power of the air, the spirit that now worketh in the children of disobedience' (Eph. 2:2), but also as 'the god of this world' with the power to blind the minds of man so that they could not see the 'the light of the glorious gospel of Christ, who is the image of God' (2 Cor. 4:4).

Satan does everything possible here on earth to disgrace the name of God, bringing all into disobedience of God's will, and Satan's greatest desire was to ascend into heaven to do the same. For the glory of God's name and God's plan, Jesus Christ died and was resurrected instead to glorify the name of God, judging Satan and providing to all men hope and the way to fellowship with God:

> Now is the judgment of this world: now shall the prince of this world be cast out.
> And I [Jesus], if I be lifted up from the earth, will draw all men unto me. (John 12:31-32)

Jesus was sent into the world...
> To open their eyes, and to turn them from darkness to light, and from the power of Satan unto God, that they may receive forgiveness of sins, and inheritance among them which are sanctified by faith that is in me (Acts 26:18).

Satan's 'I will exalt my throne above the stars of God'
In the vanity of his mind, the blindness of his heart, and desiring complete alienation from the light of God, Lucifer coveted and aspired to occupy heaven, the abode of God Himself. He coveted and aspired to exalt his throne above the 'stars of God' referring to his desire to rule all the angelic creatures. The stars visible in the sky were not what Lucifer was meaning. Instead, he was seeking to be exalted above God's angelic messengers or 'stars': for example, Revelation 1:16 and 20 describes the Lord holding the seven 'stars' in His hand which He declares to be His messengers to the churches, or, when Jehovah speaks to Job: 'Whereupon are the foundations thereof fastened? or who laid the corner stone thereof; when the morning stars sang together and all the sons of God shouted for joy?' (Job 38:6, 7).

Satan's 'I will sit upon the mount of the congregation'
Lucifer also coveted and aspired to ambitiously govern the universe and all therein by dethroning God from His royal seat over the congregation. The 'congregation' refers to more than just fallen man, it includes as the Psalmist (82:1) indicates: 'God standeth in the congregation of the mighty; he judgeth among the gods' (those chosen by God to judge on earth and heaven, see Exodus 22:9, 28; John 10:34).

Micaiah described God's congregation in heaven while prophesying to Ahab king of Israel and before Jehoshaphat king of Judah: 'Therefore hear the word of the Lord; I saw the Lord sitting upon his throne, and all the host of heaven standing on his right hand and on his left' (2 Chron. 18:18). The reference to the congregation also refers to Satan's desire for the authority to judge as God judges. Sadly, those who seek to follow Satan's desire to be exalted to the position of judge fail, as Satan failed, to recognize the warning of the king of Judah, Jehoshaphat: 'Take heed what ye do: for ye judge not for man, but for the Lord, who is with you in the judgment... Thus shall ye do in the fear of the Lord, faithfully, and with a perfect heart' (2 Chron. 19:4-6, 9).

Lucifer's will to govern the congregation speaks of his will to be exalted with the acclaim and homage of a government ruler. God's government of created beings begins with 'the holy ones' in heaven surrounding Him. In the government of heaven: 'God is greatly to be feared in the assembly of the holy ones, and to be had in reverence of all them that are about him' (Ps. 89:7).

Lucifer further describes the location of his desired government as 'in the sides of the north'. Scripture makes reference to heaven's government being located to the north of earth as in Psalm 75:2, 6-7: 'When I shall receive the congregation I will judge uprightly ... Promotion cometh neither from the east, nor from the west, nor from the south. But God is the judge: He putteth down one, and setteth up another.'

Satan's 'I will ascend above the heights of the clouds'

Ascending above the heights of the clouds describes Satan's desire for the glory that belonged to God alone. In exaltation before His people 'the glory of the Lord appeared in the cloud' and God spoke to Moses (Exod. 16:10-11). In wrath against enemies of His people, 'The burden of Egypt. Behold, the Lord rideth upon a swift cloud, and shall come into Egypt ... The Lord hath mingled a perverse spirit in the midst thereof: and they have caused Egypt to err in every work thereof, as a drunken man staggereth in his vomit' (Is. 19:1, 14).

The apostles were left looking upward as Christ ascended into heaven and a cloud received Him (Acts 1:9). Christ announced to the

High Priest at the time of His trial and death that He would return to earth 'coming in the clouds of heaven' (Matt. 26:64; Rev. 14:14-16). God's glory is further confirmed by St. Paul's description of the rapture of his saints: 'we which are alive and remain shall be caught up together with them [the dead in Christ] in the clouds, to meet the Lord in the air: and so shall we ever be with the Lord' (1 Thess. 4:16-17). It is above this symbol of clouds accompanying the Lord which Lucifer desired to climb.

Satan's 'I will be like the most high'
Satan's final 'I will' perfectly describes his ultimate proud desire to be 'like the most high' – the phrase in Hebrew is *El Elyon* emphasizing God's strength and sovereignty. The war declared by Satan extends down from heaven to the very nations here on earth spoken of by Moses: 'When the most High divided to the nations their inheritance' (Deut. 32:7-8). Whether being challenged by Satan or an earthly king, God will judge those who challenge His decrees, as here with the boundaries of the people of earth. In Isaiah 10:13 the Assyrian king, who is a type of Antichrist of the future, boasted: 'I have removed the bounds of the people, and have robbed their treasures; and I have put down the inhabitants like a valiant man.' The Lord through His prophet Isaiah interrupts this satanic boaster to expose His displeasure: 'When the Lord hath performed His whole work upon mount Zion and on Jerusalem, I will punish the fruit of the stout heart of the king of Assyria, and the glory of his high looks' (Is. 10:12).

God's name of *El Elyon*, as the Most High, further describes His character as 'the possessor of heaven and earth' as when Abram was blessed by Melchizedek, king of Salem, priest of 'the most high God, possessor of heaven and earth' (Gen. 14:18-19). Lucifer's ultimate goal of removing God from His throne where He possesses all of heaven and earth is further shown by Satan's choice of God's name as 'the Most High' and not one of His other names in Scripture, like: The Eternal Word, The Good Shepherd, the I AM, The Way, The Light, The Life, The Truth, The Saviour, The Redeemer, The Comforter or even The Creator. Satan could never be like the Most High because in Satan are none of the qualities of God.

Satan's evil, deceitful, hurtful qualities – be forewarned

There is no darkness with light and Satan's word creates nothing; he is a wolf in sheep's clothing seeking to desecrate God's flock; he was created after eternity past; his ways always lead to despair; his paths are of darkness and sadness; he leads all men who follow to eternal death as he has led his fallen angels; he is the father of all lies; he places the spirit of hate and bondage in men's heart who have not received the light of Christ (Rom. 8:15). His comfort lasts just a brief time until he has used you for his evil purposes, attempting always to defeat the pleasures of God. Satan will be judged for all persons he deceived and for all suffering he created and caused – Satan's destiny is agony, anguish, and tormenting terror in bondage, always in hell and forever in the lake of fire.

Satan used by God to glorify His name

Find solace and comfort in the knowledge that God allows Satan to exist to glorify God's name for all of creation to witness, especially 'them who are the called according to his purpose' (Rom. 8:28-29). God is always using Satan as Scripture 'saith unto Pharaoh, Even for this same purpose have I raised thee up, that I might shew my power in thee, and that my name might be declared throughout all the earth' (Rom. 9:17). Pray always for the grace and mercy of God to be part of the body of Christ, never high-minded because of the gifts of God, always abhorring what is evil, and being transformed to the will of God through faith in Christ (Rom. 12:2-12).

Trust in Christ, believe not Satan's lie of no eternal hell

Our trust and love must always be with Christ and His love for us. He warns us that those who instead follow the evil ways of the devil and his demonic hordes 'will suffer the punishment of eternal destruction and exclusion from the presence of the Lord and from the glory of His might, when He comes on that day to be glorified in His saints, and to be marvelled at in all who have believed' (2 Thess. 1:9). The punishment of 'eternal destruction' can be substituted with 'eternal ruin'. Pray for the faith and strength to keep your heart, mind and body always close to God's ways so His grace will favour you when judgment comes so you can enjoy eternal life and not the punishment of eternal fire:

> *Then He will say to those at His left hand, 'Depart from me, you cursed, into the eternal fire prepared for the devil and his angels.'*

And they will go away into eternal punishment, but the righteous into eternal life (Matt. 25:41, 46).

This is illustrated by the story of Abraham and the rich man in Hades who, while on earth, sought only personal enjoyment of worldly things and sought his own personal pleasure with no regard for others in need. While in Heaven Abraham describes an eternal separation with no avenue of escape: 'And besides all this, between us and you a great chasm has been fixed, in order that those who would pass from here to you may not be able, and none may cross from there to us' (Luke 16:26). We are told repeatedly to trust the Word of God and, with the prayerful help of the Holy Spirit and the holy ministering angels, refuse to follow Satan. St. Paul makes this warning clear:

> For God will render to every man according to his works: to those who by patience in well-doing seek for glory and honour and immortality, He will give eternal life; but for those who are factious and do not obey the truth, but obey wickedness, there will be wrath and fury (Rom. 2:6-8).

We should heed God's warning to Samuel when he was sent by the Lord to Jesse the Beth-lehemite to find 'a king among his sons' whom God had provided; '... the Lord said unto Samuel, Look not on his countenance, or on the height of his stature; ... for the Lord seeth not as man seeth; for man looketh on the outward appearance, but the Lord looketh on the heart' (1 Sam. 16:1, 7). As 'Samuel took the horn of oil, and anointed David in the midst of his brethren: and the Spirit of the Lord came upon David from that day forward' (1 Sam. 16:13). And as David's heart was pure in the Lord, if our hearts are pure in Christ we also will be anointed of the oil of the Holy Spirit who will dwell within us.

Chapter 25

Through Christ Stand Strong against Satan and His Demonic Horde

The whole armour of God

All of the devastation around us is not caused by our Lord but rather is caused by Satan and his demons. We must seek God's Word for direction. We can only stand against 'the wiles of the devil' by putting on the whole armour of God: 'For we wrestle not against flesh and blood, but against principalities, against powers, against the rulers of the darkness of this world, against spiritual wickedness in high places' (Eph. 6:12). In fact we are commanded to put on the whole armour of God, being told this is all we can do so we may withstand the evil (Eph. 6:13). Never forget that, as believers in Christ, we have enemies in the demonic hosts of Satan, always assembled for mortal combat. Scripture elaborates upon the whole armour of God:

> Stand therefore, having your loins girt about with truth, and having on the breastplate of righteousness;
> And your feet shod with the preparation of the gospel of peace;
> Above all, taking the shield of faith, wherewith ye shall be able to quench all the fiery darts of the wicked.
> And take the helmet of salvation, and the sword of the Spirit, which is the word of God:
> Praying always with all prayer and supplication in the Spirit, and watching thereunto with all perseverance and supplication for all saints (Eph. 6:14-18).

The armour of God consists of: (1) having your loins girt about with truth which holds everything together and refers to the believer's integrity; (2) having on the breastplate of righteousness with the knowledge that righteousness practised by the believer protects the chest and heart from Satan; (3) having your feet shod with the preparation of the gospel of peace, the sharing of which brings joy to the heart of God and gives your lives support and stability; (4) having the shield of faith in hand to quench all the fiery darts (spears or lance) of the wicked; (5) having the helmet of salvation on your head guarding your mind and thoughts from the wickedness of spiritual influences; and, (6) having the 'sword of the spirit' which is the Word of God as the only offensive tool necessary, having the Word always in your heart and on your lips. Too often when this Scripture is spoken the last command in verse 18 is overlooked: 'Praying always with all prayer and supplication in the Spirit' while being persistent and directing your prayers for all believers since all are targets of Satan's fiery darts.

The 'god of this world' who is Satan will treat you with dishonesty by using deceitful teachers to adulterate the Word of God and, with every effort, try to lead you to the edge and into his abyss of hell by subverting the spiritual shining light in your heart of the gospel of Jesus Christ (2 Cor. 4:1-6). Follow God's command to share with everyone the knowledge of the glory of God in the face of Jesus Christ, sharing even with those in darkness: 'preach the Gospel to every creature' (Mark 16:15). The god of this world has blinded the minds of them which believe not but even Satan does not know who is predestinated by God to be one of His sheep: 'God chose you from the beginning to be saved through sanctification by the Spirit' (2 Thess. 2:13). Exercise your gift of prayer on every occasion calling for God's ministering angels to watch and protect, continually in the power of the Spirit of God, focusing your call on behalf of every believer who is constantly the target of Satan's devices so the Gospel can be ever preached.

Do not let Satan slow your spreading of the Gospel to every person which shall 'be a light of the Gentiles, ... shouldest be for salvation unto the ends of the earth' (Acts 13:47; Is. 49:6). Satan may have been given great power as shown by his title 'the prince of this world' (John 12:31). And he may appear as an 'angel of light' (2 Cor. 11:14). However, the prince of this world does not know who will be glad in hearing and glorifying the Word of the Lord by their belief in Christ because they 'were ordained to eternal life' (Acts 13:48). Ignore the lies of Satan! Always preach the gospel because Jesus said: 'my sheep hear my voice, I know them, and they follow me: And I give unto them eternal life; and they shall never perish, neither shall any man pluck them out of my hand. My Father, which gave them me, is greater than all; and no man is able to pluck them out of my Father's hand' (John 10:27-30). 'He that is of God heareth God's words' (John 8:47).

'And every spirit that confesseth not that Jesus Christ is come in the flesh is not of God: and this is that spirit of antichrist ... even now already is it in the world' (1 John 4:3). We are specifically warned about these demonic false spirits of the antichrist. The Word continues: 'Ye are of God, little children, and have overcome them [these antichrist false teachers]: because greater is he that is in you, than he that is in the world... We are of God: he that knoweth God heareth us; he that is not of God heareth not us. Hereby know we the spirit of truth, and the spirit of error' (1 John 4:4, 6). We should pray for the promised gift of Christ that we become one of those spoken of who bring the truth as men sent as apostles, prophets, evangelists, pastors and teachers: 'For the perfecting of the saints, for the work of the ministry, for the edifying of the body of Christ' (Ephesians 4:11, 12).

Those of God 'have an unction from the Holy One, and ye know all things' meaning his sheep have been anointed by the Holy Spirit and thus can discern between truth and error (1 John 2:20). Never believe the demons of the devil who would have you be silent, for God's sheep have been anointed because they are chosen of God with the Holy Spirit's power teaching them 'all things' with no need of 'any man [to] teach you' (1 John 2:27). Trust God for He knows which are His chosen and which are not, 'And these are they by the way side, where the word is sown; but when they have heard, Satan cometh immediately, and taketh away the word that was sown in their hearts' (Mark 4:15). Do not judge yourselves as to whom you should bring the good news and to whom you extend a helping hand: 'Let brotherly love continue. Be not forgetful to entertain strangers: for thereby some have entertained angels unawares' (Heb. 13:1-2).

Know this always: Satan is a liar, always has been, and will continue to strive to steal God's promised salvation from His children in an attempt to murder their body and spirits. 'Ye are of your father the devil, and the lusts of your father ye will do. He was a murderer from the beginning, and abode not in the truth, because there is no truth in him. When he speaketh a lie, he speaketh of his own: for he is a liar, and the father of it' (John 8:44). While preaching the Gospel of Jesus Christ pray earnestly for strength from God's angels and the Holy Spirit knowing with confidence 'the God of peace shall bruise Satan under your feet shortly. The grace of our Lord Jesus Christ be with you. Amen' (Rom. 16:20).

Satan will attempt in all ways to cause man to rebel against the will of God. The evil spirits of Satan, his demonic hordes, speak lies of hypocrisy and are always trying to convince us to murmur. Refuse to complain, instead always give thanksgiving, knowing the truth of God and His Son (1 Tim. 4:1-3). The will of God is an unbending straight line of truth and goodness. God's will is ever moving with absolute certainty across the universe of space, time and thought. Sin can be defined as any variation from the will of God, even if it be of the slightest degree of variation. John the Baptist cried as 'the voice in the wilderness, Make straight the way of the Lord, as said the prophet Esaias' (John 1:23).

Remember that our war is not always with what is seen:

> For though we walk in the flesh, we do not war after the flesh;
> (For the weapons of our warfare are not carnal, but mighty through God to the pulling down of strong holds;)
> Casting down imaginations, and every high thing that exalteth itself against the knowledge of God, and bringing into captivity every thought to the obedience of Christ;
> And having in a readiness to revenge all disobedience, when your obedience is fulfilled (2 Cor. 10:3-6).

You can trust in the results of daily putting on the whole armour of God. In the end, and within you, Christ shall put down all rule and all authority and power that is not of God; For He must reign until He hath put all enemies under His feet (1 Cor. 15:24, 25). Pray you are chosen of Christ in whom God plants eternal life, made partakers of the divine nature, having escaped the corruption that is in the world through wanting one's own way (2 Pet. 1:4). If the Bible teaches us anything, it is that in the end only God's will shall prevail.

God speaks to us with a still small voice

We are shown one of the great truths about how God works in men who seek Him. Perhaps the truth is more as to where men should be looking and listening. We are told in 1 Kings 19 Elijah stood upon the mount and 'the Lord passed by'. Elijah was looking earnestly for God as: 'a great and strong wind rent the mountains, and brake in pieces the rocks' then 'after the wind an earthquake' shook the earth, and finally 'a fire' passed by Elijah; but, God was in none of these mighty, powerful and dramatic events; instead, God revealed Himself by 'a still small voice' (1 Kgs. 19:11-13). When we are looking and listening in all earnest for our prayers' answers we should be listening for 'a still small voice'. The ways of the Most High God are not the ways of men.

Chapter 26

Satan's Judgments are From Before the Beginning of Man to the End of Time

Satan's final judgment will not come until he is cast forever into the lake of fire (Rev. 20:10). We are living in a time after Satan's position was terminated in God's government. God still permits him access to heaven (Job 1:6) where he accuses the brethren. The middle of the tribulation period will find Satan being cast from heaven and restricted to earth (Rev. 20:1-3). With Jesus' reign at his second coming at the beginning of the Millennium, Satan will be cast into the shaft of the abyss (Rev. 20:1-3) only to be loosed for a 'short time' at the end of the Millennium (Rev. 20:1-7), then cast forever into the lake of fire (Rev. 20:10).

Satan's several judgments from God and Christ Jesus have and will occur for the glory of the Lord's name: (1) his removal from guarding the throne of God (Ezek. 28:14, 16); (2) the prophecy in the garden of Eden (Gen. 3:15); (3) his defeat at the Cross (John 12:31); (4) his being barred from heaven and cast into the earth and sea (Rev. 12:9); (5) his confinement in the abyss ('bottomless pit') (Rev. 20:3); and, (6) his torment in the lake of fire forever (Rev. 20:10).

Perfection to chaos: to punish Lucifer's rebellion God's creation suffers wrath

'In the beginning God created the heavens and earth' (Gen. 1:1). Across an unknown time period, somewhere from one day to ten to fifteen billion years the second verse found in the King James Version of Scripture describes the change from perfection to desolation: 'And the earth was without form and void, and darkness covered the face of the deep' (Gen. 1:2).

Seeking further the appropriate understanding of God's wrath between verses 1 and 2, the revisers of both the English and American Bible revisions have given us instead of 'without form and void', the translation from Hebrew 'waste and void'. Verse 2 has been translated using the words of 'without form', 'void', 'waste', 'desolate', 'empty', 'wreck', and 'ruin'. Genesis 1:1-2 may be phrased thus: 'In the beginning God created the heavens and earth. And the earth by God's wrath became a wreck and a ruin, and darkness covered the face of the deep.' Do not allow confusion to enter the analysis by failing to distinguish the vast difference between the original creation of the heavens and earth, and the later formation, fashioning and restoration of that same earth which had been turned into chaos.

To 'create' in Genesis 1:1 is to produce out of nothing whereas Isaiah 45:18 distinguishes: 'Thus saith the Lord that created the heavens; God himself that formed the earth and made it; he hath **established** it, he created it not a chaos, he **formed** it to be inhabited: I am the Lord; and there is none else.' Furthermore, if we substitute the translated verb as it is in its precise form from Genesis 19:26: 'Lot's wife looked back and she **became** a pillar of salt' we legitimately read Genesis 1:2 as: 'And the earth **became** without form and void.'

Satan's rebellion led to the first judgment upon earth

In fact, the Scripture is consistent in all of God's nature of hatred against sin and His pouring out His wrath upon all ungodliness. God's curse issued forth against the creation corrupted by sin beginning with Genesis 1:2 at a time in all likelihood when Lucifer made his famous decision to oppose God's will. Not only does the catastrophe of God's wrath extend to earth but to the heavens above, the first and second heavens, suffered their own judgment. Jeremiah declares the heavens had no light (4:23), and Job says the light of the sun and stars was shut off from the earth (Job 9:7).

Satan's kingdom suffered total chaos as the earth quickly and violently was shaken: 'Which removeth the mountains, and they know not: which overturneth them in his anger. Which shaketh the earth out of her place, and the pillars [axis poles?] thereof tremble [shaken from true to magnetic?]. Which commandeth the sun, and it riseth not; and sealeth up the stars' (Job 9:5-7). Beyond the evidence of the glaciers covering the earth, geologists have discovered the total disarray of the various layers of earth literally tossed to and fro: 'Then the earth shook and trembled; the foundations also of the hills moved and were shaken, because He was wroth ... He bowed the heavens also, and came down: and darkness was under His feet... Then the channels of water were seen, and the foundations of the world were discovered at thy rebuke, O Lord at the blast of the breath of thy nostrils' (Ps. 18:7-15). Oh, how violent yet wonderfully gentle God's breath can be, comparing His breath of wrath with His breath of life: 'the Lord God formed man of the dust of the ground, and breathed into his nostrils the breath of life; and man became a living soul' (Gen. 2:7).

Jeremiah describes God's creation becoming chaos (does it describe the second verse of Genesis?):

I beheld the earth, and, lo, it was without form, and void; and the heavens, and they had no light.

I beheld the mountains, and, lo, they trembled, and all the hills moved lightly.

I beheld, and, lo, there was no man, and all the birds of heaven were fled.

I beheld, and, lo, the fruitful place was a wilderness, and all the cities thereof were broken down at the presence of the Lord, and by His fierce anger.

For thus hath the Lord said, The whole land shall be desolate; yet will I not make a full end.

For this shall the earth mourn, and the heavens above be black: because I have spoken it, I have purposed it, and will not repent, neither will I turn back from it (Jer. 4:23-28).

God did not create the earth in chaos; 'as for God his way is perfect' (Ps. 18:30). 'The words of the Lord are pure words: as silver tried in a furnace of earth, purified seven times' (Ps. 12:6).

Thus saith God the Lord, he that created the heavens, and stretched them out; he that spread forth the earth, and that which cometh out of it; he that giveth breath unto the people upon it, and spirit to them that walk therein ... (Is. 42:5).

For thus saith the Lord that created the heavens; God himself that formed the earth and made it; he hath established it, he created it not in vain, he formed it to be inhabited: I am the Lord; and there is none else. I have not spoken in secret, in a dark place of the earth: I said not unto the seed of Jacob, Seek ye me in vain: I the Lord speak righteousness, I declare things that are right (Is. 45:18-19).

Earth continues to be cursed because of sin

The ground was cursed when Adam sinned (Gen. 3:17). When the race of man was nearly overcome with demon possession the flood came (Gen. 6:4-7). Our present age shall end and its ending is announced by the Great Tribulation (Matt. 24:21). The world itself must be purified from its accumulated sin and is to burn with fire at the end of time (2 Pet. 3:7-10). Do not forget the end time judgment of Satan in the lake of fire (Rev. 20:10) This will also involve all who chose to persevere in following him and his wicked ways (Matt. 25:41).

As true followers of Christ we should be comforted by God's patience and grace for purposes His own. God is longsuffering so that none may perish.

Chapter 27

Angels Which Kept Not Their First Estate And Sinned

God did not spare 'the angels that sinned' and he 'cast them down to hell, and delivered them into chains of darkness, to be reserved unto judgment' (2 Pet. 2:4). The 'angels that sinned' can be referring to possibly the fallen angels who sinned grievously by cohabitating with women as described in Genesis 6:1-5 (an attempt by Satan to pollute the blood line of 'the woman' to defeat the prophecy to Satan in the garden by God concerning his outcome by 'the woman'). Or, the 'angels that sinned' may refer to angels who rebelled with Satan before Adam and Eve sinned in the garden.

These sinning angels were placed by God into hell or Tartarus. In either case, these angels are further described in Jude 6 as 'the angels which kept not their first estate'. We should keep in mind that some evil angels, the demons, are still free and doing Satan's will here on earth.

Whenever you encounter someone who teaches a different Gospel than that of the risen Christ as taught by Scripture, remember the context of both 2 Peter 2:4 and Jude 6 – that as God so punishes angels surely He will punish false teachers. Also, remember in the last days upon our return to earth as glorified saints 'we shall judge [the fallen] angels' (1 Cor. 6:3).

Chapter 28

Satan's Defeat at the Cross

Satan is defeated as explained in the Scripture by Jesus' conquest over 'the prince of this world' who shall be cast out once Jesus is lifted up from the earth drawing all men unto himself. Jesus made this statement in response to an angel who spoke to him in a voice from heaven saying to all there: 'I have both glorified it, and will glorify it again.' Jesus' first response to the angel's voice is to tell the men with him, including his apostles, Pharisees and certain Greeks: 'This voice came not because of me, but for your sakes' (John 12:28-32).

'The prince of this world is judged' Jesus proclaims to His disciples while telling them of the coming Comforter: 'Howbeit when he, the Spirit of truth, is come, he will guide you into all truth: for he shall not speak of himself; but whatsoever he shall hear, that shall he speak: and he will shew you things to come. He shall glorify me: for he shall receive of mine, and shall shew it unto you. All things that the Father hath are mine: therefore said I, that he shall take of mine, and shall shew it unto you' (John 16:11, 13-15).

Beyond being judged, Satan and his dominions are openly defeated:

[Be] comforted, being knit together in love, and unto all riches of the full assurance of understanding, to the acknowledgment of the mystery of God, and of the Father, and of Christ;
    In whom are hid all the treasures of wisdom and knowledge. And this I say, lest any man should beguile you with enticing words. (Col 2:2-4)

As ye have therefore received Christ Jesus the Lord, so walk ye in him:...

Beware lest any man spoil you through philosophy and vain deceit, after the tradition of men, after the rudiments of the world, and not after Christ.
For in him dwelleth all the fulness of the Godhead bodily.
And ye are complete in him, which is the head of all principality and power: (Col.2:6, 8-10)

Blotting out the handwriting of ordinances that was against us, which was contrary to us, and took it out of the way, nailing it to his cross;
And having spoiled principalities and powers, he made a shew of them openly, triumphing over them in it. (Col 2:14-15)

Let no man beguile you of your reward in a voluntary humility and worshipping of angels, intruding into those things which he hath not seen, vainly puffed up by his fleshly mind (Col. 2: 18).

Chapter 29

Angels: God Created Free-willed Beings Who Can Rebel

Job 1 and 2 makes clear that Satan, as well as the other angels created by God, is an individual and personal spirit being, not just an evil influence. Satan has intellect as demonstrated by his conversing with the Lord. Satan has emotions demonstrated by his antagonism towards Job (Job 1:9-11). Satan's will is demonstrated by his purpose to destroy Job and disgrace God (Job 1:11; 2:4-5, 7). The Word of God consistently presents Satan as both a real person and a spirit being.

Satan's name means 'adversary', perfectly describing his basic nature as related to both God and man. Thus, Satan's nature is to be an antagonist, and to oppose God's Person, His plan and His people.

Satan had and still has access to the earth and freedom to roam around on it. He will continue to exercise this freedom of movement until he is bound for a thousand years during the Millennium (Rev. 20:2) and then cast into the lake of fire forever (Matt. 25:41). Until Satan's final judgment be wary of his wiles, for he roams the earth as a hungry lion seeking whom he can devour (1 Pet. 3:5).

Satan and all angels are limited by God's permission

'And the Lord said unto Satan, Behold, all that he hath is in thy power; only upon himself put not forth thine hand. So Satan went forth from the presence of the Lord' (Job 1:12). Thereafter Job 2:3-6 describes God giving Satan permission to test Job's perfectness, his uprightness, his fear of God, his disdain of evil and his integrity in his faith, by 'the Lord saying unto Satan, Behold, he is in thine hand; but save his life'.

Importantly, note that the omniscient Lord initiated the conversation with Satan that led to Job's being tested; and, God's Word expressly pays the highest tribute to the character of Job: 'Hast thou considered my servant Job, that there is none like him in the earth, a perfect and an upright man, one that feareth God, and escheweth evil? and still he holdeth fast his integrity, although thou movedst me against him, to destroy him without cause' (Job 2:3). In the end, Satan, as all the angels, are used of God for His glory and for His name.

Satan's dominion on earth allowed for a time

It must be remembered that Lucifer was given a throne on earth where his sphere of rule existed and still exists. God, when He created Lucifer, gave the earth as his province: Lucifer 'had been in Eden the garden of God' (Ezek. 28:22), called by Christ 'the prince of this world' (John 12:31; 14:30; 16:11), who while tempting Jesus, took Him up into a high mountain and showed unto Him all the kingdoms of the world in a moment of time offering to give all the power and glory of those kingdoms with the right of authority from God as expressed in the unchallenged words of Satan 'for that [the kingdoms of the world] is delivered unto me' (Luke 4:5-7). Isaiah 14:12 makes clear: 'How art thou fallen from heaven, O Lucifer, son of the morning! how art thou cut down to the ground, which didst weaken the nations!'

Even though Satan was 'cut down to the ground' he is still allowed to exert great power by his outward manifestations of rebellion. We are forewarned of any person, religion or angel that seeks a different will to the will of God. The will of God is truth, goodness, righteousness and holiness, which the evil in the heart of Lucifer, God's highest and most wonderfully created being in the universe, desired for his own self-gratification and edification.

God, in His infinite wisdom, chose not to destroy Lucifer and instead will allow all to see his foolhardy, pathetic and disloyal ambitions. The angels have already witnessed the emptiness of Lucifer's desires and claims of his own glory as described between the times of Genesis 1:1 and 1:2, but man has yet to see the true extent of God's judgment upon Lucifer's 'I will' rebellion.

Chapter 30

Hell's Eternal Punishment of Satan, Demons, and All the Wicked

The New Testament makes a full revelation and disclosure principally by Jesus Christ who describes the outlook into the tremendous future of hell. The suffering in Hades and Gehenna is described as: 'everlasting punishment' (Matt. 25:46); 'everlasting fire' (Matt. 18:8); 'the fire that never shall be quenched' (Mark 9:45); 'the worm that dieth not' (Mark 9:46); 'flaming fire' (2 Thess. 1:8); 'everlasting chains' (Jude 6); 'eternal fire' (Jude 7); 'the blackness of darkness for ever' (Jude 13); 'the smoke of torment ascending up for ever and ever' (Rev. 14:11; 19:3); 'the lake of fire and brimstone', in which the devil, the beast and the false prophet 'shall be tormented day and night, for ever and ever' (Rev. 20:10).

The punishment of the wicked is more properly 'endless' than eternal. The description 'everlasting' is of prime importance. To determine its meaning as applied to the punishment of the wicked it is required to first determine the substantive from which the adjective is derived: 'ever' signifies an 'age'. This is a time-word. 'Age' denotes 'duration', more or less. The word 'duration' or 'age' does not determine, standing alone, the length of the duration or age. For example, God has duration, and angels have duration. The Creator has 'age', and the creature has 'age'; but the 'age' of the creature is nothing compared with that of the Creator. 'Behold thou hast made my days as handbreath; and mine age is as nothing before thee' (Ps. 39:5).

As to man and his existence the Scriptures speak of two and only two 'ages': one limited, and one endless; the latter succeeding the former; and, one finite, and one infinite.

Scripture mentions the two 'ages' together repeatedly: 'It shall not be forgiven him, neither in this world ("age"), nor in the world ("age") to come' (Matt. 12:32); 'He shall receive an hundred-fold now in this time, and in the world ("age") to come, eternal life' (Mark 10:30); 'He shall receive manifold more in this present time, and in the world ("age") to come, life everlasting' (Luke 18:30); 'Above every name that is named, not only in this world ("age"), but also in that which is to come' (Eph. 1:21).

Eternity is relative and not absolute. Compare the usage of 'things present' and the 'things to come', mentioned in Romans 8:38 and 1 Corinthians 3:22. The future 'age' has a beginning but no ending. This is the meaning of the common phrase 'a man has gone into eternity' and that a man's happiness or misery is 'eternal'. The eternity of God is separate, as an absolute eternity has no beginning as well as no ending. However, the eternity or immortality of men or angels or other created beings is a relative eternity with a beginning but no end. Scripture designates the absolute eternity of God by the description, 'from everlasting to everlasting' (Ps. 90:2). The time for any opportunity for God's forgiveness is during this present 'age' during our time in the world while 'things present' exist. 'Hath never forgiveness' speaks to a miserable time of no ending and no further choices; see for example:

> Jesus teaches: 'But he that shall blaspheme against the Holy Ghost hath never forgiveness, but is in danger of eternal damnation' (Mark 3:29).

> St. Peter describes the punishment of false teachers who bring 'damnable heresies, even denying the Lord that bought them, and bring upon themselves swift destruction' (v.2) as being 'to whom the mist of darkness is reserved for ever (v.17). 'Mists of darkness' literally means gloom of darkness meaning eternal torment (2 Pet. 2:2, 17).

> Jude, the half brother of Jesus, described the punishment of false teachers in verse 6 as that of 'the angels which kept not their first estate' and as involving restraint 'in everlasting chains under darkness unto the judgment of the great day' and further

describing the punishment in verse 13 using the comparison of shooting stars into the abyss of outer space as 'to whom is reserved the blackness of darkness for ever' (Jude 6 and 13).

Judgments of God and angels' warning not to look back

Sodom and Gomorrah were destroyed by fire and brimstone for the peoples' wickedness, including rampant and open homosexuality. Before the destruction of the two cities Abraham had received visitors, including the LORD and two angels, who were offered food and drink (Gen. 18:1-8). Before the two angels went off to Sodom to retrieve Lot, the Lord gave Abraham and Sarah the good news of being blessed with a son next year when He promised to return (Gen. 18:10). Abraham then attempted to save the people of Sodom during the famous bargain that ended with God's agreement the city would be saved if ten righteous men were found in the city (Gen. 18:23-33).

The judgment against these two cities came, as the Lord said: 'Because the cry of Sodom and Gomorah is great, and because their sin is very grievous' (Gen. 18:18-20). Due to the evil designs of the men of Sodom to homosexually rape the two angels who had gone to Lot, the angels 'smote the men that were at the door of Lot's house with blindness, both small and great: so that they wearied themselves to find the door' (Gen. 19:11).

Sodom's wicked pull was great, causing Lot to procrastinate in leaving. 'The Lord being merciful unto Lot' had the angels physically take Lot, his wife and two daughters by their hands leading them out of the city (Gen. 19:15-16). After the angels brought Lot and his family to safety 'the Lord rained upon Sodom and upon Gomorrah brimstone and fire from the Lord out of heaven; And he overthrew those cities, and all the plain, and all the inhabitants of the cities, and that which grew upon the ground' (Gen. 19:24-25). Sadly, Lot's wife longed for the sinful city life, disobeying the angels' warning by looking back, and was judged by becoming a pillar of salt (Gen. 19:26).

Herod's pride and judgment

The sin judged in Sodom was open and rampant. However, we should also learn the lesson of the inward sin of pride exemplified by King Herod's judgment. Judgment for his open violence against the apostles had been withheld: Herod had just James killed and was planning to kill Peter who was saved when the angel released him from prison (Acts 12:1-19). From Herod we should learn that it is sinful for any of us not to give all glory to God and instead act vainly and with pride thinking, even for a moment, we are raised to divine status. Scripture describes Herod's sin:

> Herod arrayed in royal apparel, sat upon his throne, and made an oration unto them [the representatives of Tyre and Sidon].
> And the people gave a shout, saying, It is a voice of a god, and not of a man.
>   And immediately the angel of the Lord smote him, because he gave not God the glory: and he was eaten of worms, and gave up the ghost (Acts 12:21-23).

From the immediate judgment of Herod by the angel of the Lord, it is clear Herod had vainly agreed in his heart with the people who shouted he spoke as 'a god'. Herod's heart spoke loudly to God's ears, as the words of our heart are heard by God (Ps. 34:15, 17).

Tribulation martyrs clothed in white linen praising the Lamb
God will honour those who accept His loving grace and surrender their own pride for the glory of God. During the end time Tribulation period, the time of wrath, many will surrender their will to God, refusing to accept the mark of the beast and worship the Antichrist Devil. Many will escape the 'wrath of the Lamb' by standing in faith in Jesus Christ as their personal Saviour. Those who do stand in faith will die at the order of the Antichrist. These martyred tribulation saints will honour God and be honoured in heaven at the throne of God.

During the Great Tribulation in heaven 'all the angels' will be standing around God's throne with the elders, and the four beasts, when they all fall 'before the throne on their faces, worshipping God, Saying, Amen: Blessing, and glory, and wisdom, and thanksgiving, and honour, and power, and might, be unto our God for ever and ever. Amen' (Rev. 7:11-12). Also in heaven will be **a great multitude, which no man could number,** of all nations, and kindreds, and people, and tongues' 'clothed with white robes, and palms in their hands' 'standing before the throne and before the Lamb' all crying 'with a loud voice, saying, Salvation to our God which sitteth upon the throne, and unto the Lamb' (Rev. 7:9-10). John in the book of Revelation is given an answer by one of the elders to the questions: 'What are these which are arrayed in white robes? and whence came they?' (Rev. 7:13-14).

These are they which came out of great tribulation, and have washed their robes, and made them white in the blood of the Lamb.

Therefore are they before the throne of God, and serve him day and night in his temple: and he that sitteth on the throne shall dwell among them.

They shall hunger no more, neither thirst any more; neither shall the sun light on them, nor any heat.

For the Lamb which is in the midst of the throne shall feed them, and shall lead them unto living fountains of waters: and God shall wipe away all tears from their eyes (Rev. 7:14-17).

God will also honour the martyred saints during the Great Tribulation who refuse to accept the will of Satan. His martyred saints will be honoured by God's acceptance of their prayers just after the seventh seal and as the seven angels prepare to sound the seven trumpet judgments:

And when he had opened the seventh seal, there was silence in heaven about the space of half an hour.

And I saw the seven angels which stood before God; and to them were given seven trumpets.

And another angel came and stood at the altar, having the golden censer; and there was given unto him much incense, that he should offer it with the prayers of all saints upon the golden altar which was before the throne.

And the smoke of the incense, which came with the prayers of the saints, ascended up before God out of the angel's hand.

And the angel took the censer, and filled it with fire of the altar, and cast it into the earth: and there were voices, and thunderings, and lightnings, and an earthquake.

And the seven angels which had the seven trumpets prepared themselves to sound (Rev. 8:1-6).

Those persons left on earth who have still refused to accept the Gospel during the Great Tribulation receive this judgment emanating from the censer which had been emptied of the martyred saints' prayers and filled with the fire of the altar. Scripture is not clear whether the 'fire of the altar' cast into the earth causing 'thunderings, and lightnings, and an earthquake' will be God's answer to the prayers which have just before 'ascended up before God out of the angel's hand'.

End time angels and the pride of man

One example of the righteous judgments during the Great Tribulation time should be sufficient to show that the angels carry out the judgments against the wicked for the Lord:

And the third angel poured out his vial upon the rivers and fountains of waters; and they became blood.

And I heard the angel of the waters say, Thou are righteous, O Lord, which art, and wast, and shalt be, because thou hast judged thus.

For they have shed the blood of saints and prophets, and thou hast given them blood to drink; for they are worthy.

And I heard another cry out of the altar say, Even so, Lord God Almighty, true and righteous are thy judgments (Rev. 16:4-7).

God's judgments against the men and women during the Great Tribulation are called true and righteous because God has done everything possible for all to receive His saving grace through His Son Jesus Christ. The angels play an important part of preaching the Gospel message only as the last and final opportunity before the second coming of Jesus; no man will be able to say he had not heard about the Saviour Christ:

And I saw another angel fly in the midst of heaven, having the everlasting gospel to preach unto them that dwell on the earth, and to every nation, and kindred, and tongue, and people,

Saying with a loud voice, Fear God, and give glory to him; for the hour of his judgment is come: and worship him that made heaven, and earth, and the sea, and the fountains of waters (Rev. 14:6-7).

Even after every opportunity to accept Christ as their Saviour and Lord, those not of God will refuse to worship. It seems almost inconceivable that anyone would not receive Jesus and worship Him as their Saviour after an angel travels across all the earth preaching from the sky the Gospel to *every* man and woman; yet, some men's hearts are so hardened and wicked they insist upon seeking their own glory, refusing to bow their knee.

For all of those in the end times who are identified as 'the tares who are the children of the wicked one' Jesus says: 'The Son of Man shall send forth his angels, and they shall gather out of his kingdom all things that offend, and them which do iniquity; And shall cast them into a furnace of fire: there shall be wailing and gnashing of teeth' (Matt. 13:38-42). Truly, the judgment will come: 'When the Son of man shall come in his glory, and all the holy angels with him, then shall he sit upon the throne of his glory' (Matt 25:31).

For those men who are too proud to surrender themselves to God; for those men who are too proud to bow down to Jesus; for those men who are too proud to confess to Christ; Scripture makes very clear: 'For it is written, As I live, saith the Lord, every knee shall bow to me, and every tongue shall confess to God' (Rom. 14:11; quoting Is. 45:23). 'Wherefore God also hath highly exalted him, and given him a name which is above every name: That at the name of Jesus every knee should bow, of things in heaven, and things in earth, and things under the earth; And that every tongue should confess that Jesus Christ is Lord, to the glory of God the Father' (Phil. 2:9-11).

Chapter 31

Works of God are from God for His Glory Alone

Jesus warns us all not to become proud of the acts we do in His name by way of the story of the return of the seventy whom He sent out to the various cities to proclaim 'the Kingdom of God is come nigh unto you' with the warning that: 'I send you forth as lambs among wolves' (Luke 10:1-17). When the seventy returned they were excited to tell Jesus that 'even the devils are subject unto us through thy name'. Most tellingly, Jesus warns them first of the results of the pride of Satan and where their rejoicing should be:

> I beheld Satan as lightening fall from heaven.
> Behold, I give unto you power to tread on serpents and scorpions, and over all the power of the enemy: and nothing shall by any means hurt you.
> Notwithstanding in this rejoice not, that the spirits are subject unto you; but rather rejoice, because your names are written in heaven (Luke 10:17-20).

Notice that Jesus' immediate response is His remembrance of seeing 'Satan fall as lightening'. This refers to when Satan fell from heaven to earth when God cast him from heaven. The fall was solely due to Satan's proud heart: 'I will ...' The warning should be clear to all walking indwelled with the Holy Spirit who successfully call upon His anointing to effect this world. We must focus our attention and thanks upon God's ultimate grace of salvation through Jesus' death at the cross and resurrection for our eternal life. Any power man has over the prince of this world and his demonic spirits is a gift from God and no doing of man. Be cautious of your pride. Instead, always focus upon the glory of God's name.

Chapter 32

Warned Not to Seek after Spirits for They are of the Devil

Seeking to make contact with the spirit world is an abomination to God. Scripture warns us 'not to learn the abominations of those nations' which can be seen today as this world's New Age movement (Deut. 18:9). The abominations are further described as 'a practicioner of witchcraft, or a soothsayer, or one who interprets omens, or a sorcerer, or one who conjures spells, or a medium, or a spiritist, or one who calls up the dead' (Deut. 18:10-11). The Lord God has directed that His children are to listen to His prophets if they are to be blameless before the Lord their God. God's wrath has been brought down upon peoples who listened to soothsayers and diviners by being driven out of the land because their abominations were so great in the eyes of the Lord (Deut. 18:12-15; cf 1 Sam. 28:13-19; 31:6).

The Lord's direction to us is to speak His word continuously: 'This book of the law shall not depart out of thy mouth' (Josh. 1:8). God is pleased by our obeying and pursuing righteousness as we 'meditate' in the Word 'day and night' and 'do according to all that is written therein: for then thou shalt make thy way prosperous, and then thou shalt have good success' (Josh. 1:8). Meditate connotes a continuous pondering, musing, rereading and reading aloud of the Word (Ps. 1:2). A critical means of protection from the worldly influences is to stay in the Word daily for we are warned to 'enter not into the path of the wicked, and go not in the way of evil men' (Prov. 4:14). Honour God by your daily meditation in His Word; you can then expect His promise: 'Have not I commanded thee? Be strong and of a good courage; be not afraid, neither be thou dismayed: for the Lord thy God is with thee whithersoever thou goest' (Josh. 1:9).

Today's New Age believers would have us deny the Word of God and seek after the spirits through channelling and other 'spiritual' means. Today, New Age Channelling is accepted – just look to the wife of former United States President Clinton who has spoken to the dead in the White House. Such practice of calling up the dead is an abomination to the Lord and can only bring destruction upon our nation and the individual participants (Deut. 18:10-11). Be warned not to believe the lies of the New Age gurus who will lead many away from God's holy ways: 'Now the Spirit speaketh expressly, that in the latter times some shall depart from the faith, giving heed to seducing spirits, and doctrines of devils; Speaking lies in hypocrisy; having their conscience seared with a hot iron' (1 Tim. 4:1-2).

King Saul failed to obey the commands of God to 'utterly destroy the sinners the Amalekites, and fight against them until they be consumed'. Instead of utterly destroying everything of the Amalekites Saul allowed his people to take 'the spoil, sheep and oxen, the chief of the things which should have been utterly destroyed, to sacrifice unto the Lord thy God in Gilgal' (1 Sam. 15:18, 21). The prophet Samuel challenges King Saul when he asks: 'Hath the Lord as great delight in burnt offerings and sacrifices, as in obeying the voice of the Lord?' (1 Sam. 15:22). Samuel answers: 'Behold, to obey is better than sacrifice, and to hearken than the fat of rams. For rebellion is as the sin of witchcraft, and stubbornness is as iniquity and idolatry. Because thou hast rejected the word of the Lord, he hath also rejected thee from being king' (1 Sam. 15:22-23).

Saul repented for his rebellion against the Lord before Samuel twice thereafter (1 Sam. 15:24-25, 30). Even though Samuel did turn again after Saul and Saul again worshipped the Lord, 'the Lord repented that he had made Saul king over Israel' (1 Sam. 15:31, 35). Because of Saul's sin of rebellion against God's command Saul was to be replaced as king by David; Samuel vividly explains: 'for thou hast rejected the word of the Lord, and the Lord hath rejected thee from being king over Israel. And as Samuel turned about to go away, he laid hold upon the skirt of his mantle, and it rent [tore]. And Samuel said unto him [Saul], The Lord hath rent the kingdom of Israel from thee this day, and hath given it to a neighbour of thine, that is better than thou' (1 Sam. 15:26-28).

The prophet Samuel died and King Saul had no one to turn to for God's advice on how to deal with the Philistines who had gathered to war against Israel in Shunem, located seven miles east of Megiddo. The Philistines planned to battle in the plain of Jezreel while 'Saul gathered all Israel together nearby in Gilboa' (1 Sam. 28:3-5). 'And when Saul saw the host of the Philistines, he was afraid, and his heart greatly trembled. And when Saul enquired of the Lord, the Lord answered him not, neither by dreams, nor by *Urim, nor by prophets' (1 Sam. 28:6-5). [*The Urim and Thummim were stones which were mentioned in Exodus describing the breastplate Aaron wore when going into the temple: 'And thou shalt put in the breastplate of judgment the Urim and the Thummim; and they shall be upon Aaron's heart, when he goeth in before the Lord: and Aaron shall bear the judgment of the children of Israel upon his heart before the Lord continually' (Exod. 28:30).] Instead of placing the Urim into a pouch inside a holy priest's breastplate to honour the Lord, Saul apparently was using the Urim to cast it like lots to determine God's will.

Saul had earlier complied with the law by 'putting away [removing] those that had familiar spirits, and the wizards, out of the land' (1 Sam. 28:3). However, due to his great fear when no answer was forthcoming from God on what to do about the enemy army Saul again rebelled against the law of the Lord: Saul said 'unto his servant, Seek me a woman that hath a familiar spirit, that I may go to her, and enquire of her. And his servants said to him, Behold there is a woman that hath a familiar spirit at En-dor' (1 Sam. 28:7). The woman with a 'familiar spirit' was a witch or diviner who practised necromancy, consulting of the dead to determine the future. Saul was obviously aware that such consulting of the dead was strictly forbidden by the law. When the Lord was speaking to Moses, giving the Israelites the law, He said: 'Regard not them that have familiar spirits, neither seek after wizards, to be defiled by them: I am the Lord your God' (Lev. 19:31).

Saul came in disguise to the witch of En-dor and she called upon the dead spirit of Samuel as Saul had requested of her. The witch cried out in a loud voice when the spirit of Samuel actually appeared which she described as: 'I saw gods ascending out of the earth... An old man cometh up; and he is covered with a mantel' (1 Sam. 28:13-

14). When Samuel appeared he spoke to Saul: 'Why hast thou disquieted me, to bring me up? And Saul answered, I am sore distressed; for the Philistines make war against me, and God is departed from me, and answered me no more ... make known unto me what I shall do' (1 Sam. 28:15). Samuel gave a chilling response:

> Wherefore then dost thou ask of me, seeing the Lord is departed from thee, and is become thine enemy?
>
> And the Lord hath done to him, as he spake by me: for the Lord hath rent the kingdom out of thine hand, and given it to thy neighbour, even to David.
>
> Because thou obeyedst not the voice of the Lord, nor executedst his fierce wrath upon Amalek, therefore hath the Lord done this thing unto thee this day.
>
> Moreover the Lord will also deliver Israel with thee into the hand of the Philistines: and tomorrow shalt thou and thy sons be with me [in death]: the Lord also shall deliver the host of Israel into the hand of the Philistines (1 Sam. 28:16-19).

On the morrow, as the battle was waged, Saul was shot with the arrows of Philistine archers. Suffering serious wounds and not wanting to be captured Saul committed suicide by falling upon his sword. Samuel's words came true: 'So Saul died, and his three sons, and his armourbearer, and all his men, that same day together' (1 Sam. 31:6). Saul's rebellion against God's laws led to punishment of his family, his people, and himself.

Our modern TV version of the nice witch or the witches who today claim their constitutionally protected rights to practise their 'religion' are still an abomination before the sight of the Lord. Hollywood's embrace with movies and TV shows of approval for the New Age rebellion against the only Living God does not alter the iniquity and idolatry of practising witchcraft. Such practice is sinful and will surely be punished if there is no timely repentance before God. 'But evil men and seducers shall wax worse and worse, deceiving, and being deceived' (2 Tim. 3:13).

The Word of God can not be more clear in how we are to walk in the truth of God. We are not to sit with vain persons or go in with dissemblers [pretenders], nor be a part of the congregation of evil doers, nor sit with the wicked (Ps. 26:3-5). It is better for us to sit alone than to sit with mockers of God, those who defame the Word of God by disobeying. God will remember and visit those who suffer rebuke for His sake (Matt. 5:10-12). We are instructed to seek after and keep God's Word and make the Words of Scripture part of us, as if you 'ate them'. 'Your Word was to me the joy and rejoicing of my heart: for I am called by thy name, O Lord God of hosts' (Jer. 15:15-16). 'Be not carried about with divers and strange doctrines. Jesus Christ [is] the same yesterday, and to day, and for ever' (Heb. 13:9, 8).

Chapter 33

Demons/Devil of the Great Tribulation

During the Great Tribulation and specifically at the sixth trumpet the Scripture tells us: 'And the sixth angel sounded, and I heard a voice from the four horns of the golden altar which is before God, Saying to the sixth angel which had the trumpet, Loose the four angels which are bound in the great river Euphrates. And the four angels were loosed, which were prepared for an hour, and a day, and a month, and a year, for to slay the third part of men' (Rev. 9:13-15).

These four angels (demons?) are released in order to kill one-third of the remaining population of the earth. Added to the one-fourth who were killed under the fourth seal judgment (Rev. 6:4) these two judgments alone destroy one-half of the population, not including those who are killed by wars, famines and diseases. In verse 15 the term 'an hour' means literally 'this particular hour'. Anyone who has or will put their trust in Satan's friendship should consider how God deals with man during these last days as described in the book of Revelation.

Chapter 34

God's Wrath for Devil Worship – Holy Punishment

The Lord God foretells His people worshipping and sacrificing to devils and His consequent holy wrath.

In Deuteronomy 31:15-18 the Lord speaks to Moses after appearing in the Tabernacle 'in a pillar of a cloud: and the pillar of the cloud stood over the door of the tabernacle': saying, 'Behold, thou shalt sleep with thy fathers; and this people will rise up, and go a whoring after the gods of the strangers of the land, whither they go to be among them, and will forsake me, and break my covenant which I have made with them.' God describes how His anger will be kindled against these wicked people: 'I will forsake them, and I will hide my face from them, and they shall be devoured, and many evils and troubles shall befall them; so that they will say in that day, Are not these evils come upon us, because our God is not among us? And I will surely hide my face in that day for all the evils which they shall have wrought, in that they are turned unto other gods' (Deut. 31:17-18).

God commanded His people to bring any animal killed for food to the Tabernacle, where the blood and fat became a peace offering (Lev. 17:2-4). If any man failed to keep this commandment that man 'shall be cut off from among his people' (v.4). The command was designed to keep them from offering the blood of animals (slaughtered for food) to devils (i.e. goatlike demons), popular pagan idols of that day. God further commanded His people that 'they shall no more offer their sacrifices unto devils, after whom they have gone a whoring. This shall be a statute for ever unto them throughout their generations' (Lev. 17:7).

Beyond cutting an offender off from his people, God explains His severe and sweeping wrath towards their wilful disobedience: 'They sacrificed unto devils, not to God; to gods whom they knew not, to new gods that came newly up, whom your fathers feared not' (Deut. 32:17). The Lord God then sets forth His abhorrence because of the provoking of His sons, and of His daughters (v.19); *stating I 'will hide my face from them', chastising them as a 'forward [perverse] generation, children in whom is no faith'* (Deut. 32:19-20). God was 'provoked ... to anger with their vanities'; the 'fire kindled in His anger ... shall burn unto the lowest hell [Sheol]' consuming the earth and setting on 'fire the foundations of the mountains'; He 'will heap mischiefs upon them ... and spend his arrows upon them' (Deut. 32:21-23).

The Lord's further wrath for these sacrifices to 'devils' will lead to the sinners being 'burnt with hunger, and devoured with burning heat, and with bitter destruction: I will also send the teeth of beasts upon them, with the poison of serpents of the dust.' (Sounding much like many of the Tribulation punishments in the end times described in Revelation.) And, finally before describing the punishment of scattering His devil worshipping people, God describes the death of many: 'The sword without, and terror within, shall destroy both the young man and the virgin, the suckling also with the man of gray hairs' (Deut. 32:24-26).

The worship of devils
Jeroboam, an evil king of Israel, cast off the Priestly Levities in place of his own 'priests for the high places, and for the devils, and for the calves which he had made' (2 Chron. 11:14-15).

After learning of the ways of the heathen nations, learning their works, God's people 'served their idols', 'sacrificed their sons and daughters unto devils, and shed innocent blood, even the blood of their sons and of their daughters, whom they sacrificed unto the idols of Canaan' polluting the land 'with blood', resulting in the people being 'defiled with their own works' and 'whoring with their own inventions' and ultimately resulting in kindling the wrath of the Lord against His people 'insomuch that He abhorred His own inheritance' (Ps. 106: 35-40).

Paul warns to only fellowship with other believers at feasts and to stay away from the evils of idols and devils lest you leave yourself open for the wrath of God and demonic attacks:

> What say I then? that the idol is any thing, or that which is offered in sacrifice to idols is any thing?
>
> But I say, that the things which the Gentiles sacrifice, they sacrifice to devils, and not to God: and I would not that ye should have fellowship with devils.
>
> Ye cannot drink the cup of the Lord, and the cup of devils: ye cannot be partakers of the Lord's table, and of the table of devils.
>
> Do we provoke the Lord to jealousy? are we stronger than he? (1 Cor. 10:19-22).

The warning of God's coming wrath will go unheeded. Men in the end times will only worship devils and idols, refusing to repent of their other sinful acts.

> And the rest of the men which were not killed by these plagues, yet repented not of the works of their hands, that they should not worship devils, and idols of gold and silver, and brass, and stone, and of wood: which neither can see, nor hear, nor walk:
>
> Neither repented they of their murders, nor of their sorceries, nor of their fornication, nor of their thefts (Rev. 9:20-21).

Demon worship may involve sorceries

Chapter 9 of Revelation shows the reality of the unseen world of Satan and demons, and it shows the hardness of human hearts. Verse 20 speaks to the religion of many who worship devils, demons and idols. Verse 21 speaks to the refusal to repent of their 'sorceries' which means magical arts, potions and poisons. Our word 'pharmacies' is a derivative of the Greek word for sorceries.

Live as Satan's child of the flesh or Christ's child of the Spirit

Jesus' warnings about man's choices could not be more clear, as He again warns: 'Surely I come quickly' (Rev. 22:20). We must seek to 'Walk in the Spirit' so we will not 'fulfil the lust of the flesh' (Gal.

5:16). The Scriptures teach us to seek after God and not after the flesh. We can know by the works we produce if we are of the Spirit or flesh.

> Now the works of the flesh are manifest, which are these; Adultery, fornication, uncleanness, lasciviousness, Idolatry, witchcraft, hatred, variance, emulations, wrath, strife, seditions, heresies, Envyings, murders, drunkenness, revellings, and such like: of the which I tell you before, as I have also told you in time past, that they which do such things shall not inherit the kingdom of God.
> **But the fruit of the Spirit is love, joy, peace, longsuffering, gentleness, goodness, faith, meekness, temperance: against such there is no law.**
> And they that are Christ's have crucified the flesh with the affections and lusts. If we live in the Spirit, let us also walk in the Spirit.
> Let us not be desirous of vain glory, provoking one another, envying one another (Gal. 5:19-26).

What are your works: of the Spirit or of the flesh?

An evil lie that words mean nothing, instead let your words daily praise God

Always remember to keep the love of the Lord in your heart and on your lips continuously by daily focusing all glory on God and His righteous name. While looking back on Satan's rebellious fall from grace, Jesus warns:

> O generation of vipers, how can ye, being evil, speak good things? for out of the abundance of the heart the mouth speaketh.
> A good man out of the good treasure of the heart bringeth forth good things: and an evil man out of the evil treasure bringeth forth evil things.
> But I say unto you, That every idle word that men shall speak, they shall give account thereof in the day of judgment.
> For by thy words thou shalt be justified, and by thy words thou shalt be condemned (Matt. 12:34-37).

Satan constantly lies to us saying so quietly, yet with such frequency we come to believe, the words coming from our lips are of no real importance. As children we are taught the rhyme: 'Sticks and stones may break my bones but words will never hurt me.' Do not believe anyone who down-plays the importance of your words. To God the speech from our lips is critical and can lead you into the depths of hell.

Even so the tongue is a little member, and boasteth great things. Behold, how great a matter a little fire kindleth!
And the tongue is a fire, a world of iniquity: so is the tongue among our members, that it defileth the whole body, and setteth on fire the course of nature; and it is set on fire of hell. (Jas. 3:5-6)

But the tongue can no man tame; it is an unruly evil, full of deadly poison. (Jas. 3:8)

Who is a wise man and endued with knowledge among you? let him shew out of a good conversation his works with meekness of wisdom.
But if ye have bitter envying and strife in your hearts, glory not, and lie not against the truth.
This wisdom descendeth not from above, but is earthly, sensual, devilish.
For where envying and strife is, there is confusion and every evil work (Jas. 3:13-16).

Your words can bring you to ruin or grace. Growing in Christ means that daily we remember: 'When I was a child, I spake as a child, I understood as a child, I thought as a child: but when I became a man, I put away childish things' (1 Cor. 13:11). Without works your words are left empty. Follow the command of Jesus who told us to love others as we love ourselves: 'And now abideth faith, hope, charity, these three; but the greatest of these is charity' (1 Cor. 13:13). The word 'love' can be interchanged with 'charity' here and below.

Though I speak with the tongues of men and of angels, and have not charity, I am become as sounding brass, or a tinkling cymbal. And though I have the gift of prophecy, and understand all mysteries, and all knowledge; and though I have all faith, so that I could remove mountains, and have not charity, I am nothing.
And though I bestow all my goods to feed the poor, and though I give my body to be burned, and have not charity, it profiteth me nothing.

Charity suffereth long, and is kind; charity envieth not; charity vaunteth not itself, is not puffed up.
Doth not behave itself unseemly, seeketh not her own, is not easily provoked, thinketh no evil; Rejoiceth not in iniquity, but rejoiceth in the truth.
For now we see through a glass darkly; but then face to face: now I know in part; but then shall I know even as also I am known (1 Cor. 13:1-6, 12).

The holy angels are assigned the task of keeping record of God's righteous saints. Before our tongues speak we think, and God's angels are always with us listening to our very thoughts:

Then they that feared the Lord spake often one to another: and the Lord hearkened, and heard it, and a book of remembrance was written before him for them that feared the Lord, and that thought upon his name.
And they shall be mine, saith the Lord of hosts, in that day when I make up my jewels; and I will spare them, as a man spareth his own son that serveth him. Then shall ye return, and discern between the righteous and the wicked, between him that serveth God and him that serveth him not (Mal. 3:16-18).

Jesus will show you a more excellent way where all your deeds and words will withstand the fire of purification like gold in a furnace. Your heart and mind will be revealed, everything hidden will be known. Speak only words of truth and do only works of honour with heartfelt charity for your fellow man, seek always godly righteousness.

Unbelieving devil worshippers' judgment is sure

God, in the end times, will send His angels down to judge the wicked. St. John describes how he 'saw another angel come down from heaven, having great power' to judge Babylon which 'is become the habitation of devils' (Rev. 18:1-2). Sorceries can also mean evil deceits as below:

And a mighty angel took up a stone like a great millstone, and cast it into the sea, saying, Thus with violence shall that great city Babylon be thrown down, and shall be found no more at all.

And the light of a candle shall shine no more at all in thee [the city of Babylon], ... for thy merchants were the great men of the earth; for by thy sorceries [evil deceits] were all nations deceived.

And in her was found the blood of prophets, and of saints, and of all that were slain upon the earth (Rev. 18:21, 23-24).

But the fearful, and unbelieving, and the abominable, and murderers, and whoremongers [fornicators], and sorcerers, and idolaters, and all liars, shall have their part in the lake which burneth with fire and brimstone [sulphur]: which is the second death (Rev. 21:8).

And, behold, I [Jesus] come quickly; and my reward is with me, to give every man according as his work shall be.
I am the Alpha and Omega, the beginning and the end, the first and the last.
Blessed are they that do his commandments, that they may have right to the tree of life, and may enter in through the gates into the city.
For without are dogs and sorcerers, and whoremongers, and murderers, and idolaters, and whosoever loveth and maketh a lie.
I Jesus have sent mine angel to testify unto you these things in the churches. I am the root and the offspring of David, and the bright and morning star (Rev. 22:12-16.)

God is a jealous God whose name is Jealous

Exodus 34 speaks of the Lord's warning about His nature after telling Moses to have the people destroy the altars of the people of Canaanite:

For thou shalt worship no other god: for the Lord, whose name is Jealous, is a jealous God:

> Lest thou make a covenant with the inhabitants of the land, and they go a whoring after their gods, and do sacrifice unto their gods, and one call thee, and thou eat of his sacrifice;
> And thou take of their daughters unto thy sons, and their daughters go a whoring after their gods, and make thy sons go a whoring after their gods.

Thou shalt make thee no molten gods (Exod. 34:14-17).

The Lord makes clear His nature and planned punishment after expanding upon His Second Commandment that 'Thou shalt not make unto thee any graven image, or any likeness of any thing that is in heaven above, or that is in the earth beneath, or that is in the water under the earth' (Exod. 20:4). The Lord continues: 'Thou shalt not bow down thyself to them, nor serve them: for I the Lord thy God am a jealous God, visiting the iniquity of the fathers upon the children unto the third and fourth generation of them that hate me' (Exod. 20:5).

Will we ever trust in God's longsuffering mercy and Word?

Yes, Scripture tells us of God's jealous nature and could not be any more clear. Importantly, before Moses is given the Ten Commandments the second time '... the Lord said unto Moses, Hew thee two tables of stone like unto the first: and I will write upon these tables the words that were in the first tables, which thou brakest' (Exod. 34:1). After hewing the two tables of stone Moses went up unto the Mount Sinai early the next morning. The Lord, before warning Moses about 'visiting the iniquity of the fathers upon the children', makes clear His gracious and wonderfully patient nature:

> And the Lord descended in the cloud, and stood with him there, and proclaimed the name of the Lord.
> And the Lord passed by before him, and proclaimed, The Lord, The Lord God, merciful and gracious, longsuffering, and abundant in goodness and truth,

Keeping mercy for thousands, forgiving iniquity and transgression and sin, and that will by no means clear the guilty... (Exod. 34:5-7).

Moses was told in succinct language a self-revelation about God. He is Yahweh, the self-existent, active One, everything anyone needs in every circumstance. He is 'El', the infinitely strong one. He is gracious translated from the Hebrew, *'chen'*, to 'stoop to protect us' thus God's 'favour' is like the condescending or unmerited favour of a superior person to an inferior one. He has steadfast love which is also translated in the OT for the word for grace. *He is tender, truthful, and forgiving, yet since He is always Holy. He must punish those who sin against Him.* We should always remember the words: 'For I am the Lord your God: ye shall therefore sanctify yourselves, and ye shall be holy; for I am Holy' (Lev. 11:44).

Forsake God and He will change your glory into shame
Scripture is where we must seek the knowledge of God. In our land today God's warning rings loudly in our ears: 'My people are destroyed for lack of knowledge: because thou has rejected knowledge, I will also reject thee ... seeing thou hast forgotten the law of thy God, I will also forget thy children' (Hos. 4:6).

The warning to Israel is true today as we watch our children's vicious and wicked ways. We, just as Israel, have failed to heed the call to: 'Hear the word of the Lord.' The inhabitants of our land are in conflict with the ways of God: 'there is no truth, nor mercy, nor knowledge of God in the land. By swearing, and lying, and killing, and stealing, and committing adultery, they break out, and blood toucheth blood' (Hos. 4:1-2). 'Blood toucheth blood' is another way of describing what we are seeing across our land, 'one murder follows another, leaving a trail of blood'. If we believe in Satan's call to forsake righteousness and instead sin against God we can be assured of God's Word to 'change their glory into shame' (Hos. 4:7).

Chapter 35

Satan is a liar. Instead trust God's promised blessings

When the demons of Satan come to you seeking for you to conform to this world, telling you to seek your own glory by seeking physical pleasures and denying God you should respond with what the Word says. One of the first things you will be told by these demons is that the Bible is of no importance in this modern day. Satan will try everything possible to convince you that time spent reading and mediating upon the Word of God is a waste, foolishness, and definitely too difficult to understand anyway. When you hear this evil power directing you to seek your own understanding for your conduct and thinking, command Satan to depart from you and speak these words: 'Trust in the Lord with all thine heart; and lean not unto thine own understanding. In all thy ways acknowledge him, and he shall direct thy paths' (Prov. 3:5-6). Remember Jesus' warning: 'Beware of false prophets, which come to you in sheep's clothing, but inwardly they are ravening wolves' (Matt. 7:15). Satan seeks only your destruction, no matter how nicely he dresses up his words.

Do not stop there; tell Satan and his demonic horde he is already judged and you, as one of God's children, are claiming God's blessings by always seeking His Word and ways. Tell Satan: God cannot lie, and I trust in God's promises of spiritual and physical blessing by daily searching the Scriptures which are an inspiration from God's very mouth:

My son, if thou wilt receive my words, and hide my commandments with thee; So that thou incline thine ear unto wisdom, and apply thine heart to understanding;
    Yea, if thou criest after knowledge, and liftest up thy voice for understanding; If thou seekest her as silver, and searchest for her

as for hid treasures; Then shalt thou understand the fear of the Lord, and find the knowledge of God.

For the Lord giveth wisdom: out of his mouth cometh knowledge and understanding (Prov. 2:1-6).

This book of the law shall not depart out of thy mouth; but thou shalt meditate therein day and night, that thou mayest observe to do according to all that is written therein: for then thou shalt make thy way prosperous, and then thou shalt have good success.

Have not I commanded thee? Be strong and of a good courage; be not afraid, neither be thou dismayed: for the Lord thy God is with thee whithersoever thou goest (Josh. 1:8-9).

Blessed is the man that walketh not in the counsel of the ungodly, nor standeth in the way of sinners, nor sitteth in the seat of the scornful.

But his delight is in the law of the Lord; and in his law doth he meditate day and night.

And he shall be like a tree planted by the rivers of water, that bringeth forth his fruit in his season; his leaf also shall not wither; and whatsoever he doeth shall prosper. (Ps.1:1-3)

For the Lord knoweth the way of the righteous: but the way of the ungodly shall perish (Ps. 1: 6).

Heed the warning of your worldly persecution

Angels are working for every true believer in Jesus Christ. God's highest will for us is promoted by the angelic hosts of heaven. Angels are eagerly watching us as we seek our way in the world: 'for we are made a spectacle unto the world, and to angels, and to men' (1 Cor. 4:9). Paul warns us of the treatment we should expect in the world; and, most of us will need an angel to guide our Christ-like reactions and responses to the world's treatment of those of us who call ourselves Christians:

We are fools for Christ's sake, but ye are wise in Christ; we are weak, but ye are strong; ye are honourable, but we are despised.

Even unto this present hour we both hunger, and thirst, and are naked, and are buffeted, and have no certain dwelling-place;
And labour, working with our own hands: being reviled, we bless; being persecuted, we suffer it: Being defamed, we intreat: we are made as the filth of the world, and are the offscouring of all things unto this day.
I write not these things to shame you, but as my beloved sons I warn you (1 Cor. 4:10-14).

God's angelic powers will encourage and strengthen us if we seek the face of God. Pray for guidance from your assigned angels. Stay in the Word of God and angels will encamp about us, superintending and overseeing our path through this world. Amen.

EPILOGUE

The Resurrection

The claim that Jesus rose from the dead is the key fact of the Christian faith (Matt. 28:6). 'And if Christ be not raised, your faith is vain; ye are in your sins,' wrote Paul (1 Cor. 15:17). The apostles had no doubt Jesus had risen from the dead, as He said He would. They had seen Him, spoken to Him, touched Him, watched Him appear and finally watched Him ascend into the clouds of the sky: this to them was the best evidence. The Bible lists many people who had the wondrous privilege of seeing the risen Christ (1 Cor. 15:1-8).

After experiencing the resurrected Jesus, the apostles were transformed overnight from being a weak and cowardly bunch into being a fearless group of people who preached and performed miracles in the power of their risen Lord. Each apostle was prepared to die before forsaking Jesus the Risen Christ.

The apostles had the utmost belief, trust and faith that the Word of the Lord which had been from the beginning of time was the Lord Jesus Himself:

In the beginning was the Word, and the Word was with God, and the Word was God. The same was in the beginning with God. All things were made by him; and without him was not any thing made that was made. In him was life; and the life was the light of men. And the light shineth in darkness; and the darkness comprehended it not.

[The Word] was the true Light, which lighteth every man that cometh into the world. He was in the world, and the world was made by him, and the world knew him not. He came unto his own, and his own received him not.

But as many as received him, to them gave he power to become the sons of God, even to them that believe on his name: Which were born, not of blood, nor of the will of the flesh, nor of the will of man, but of God.

And the Word was made flesh, and dwelt among us, (and we beheld his glory, the glory as of the only begotten of the Father,) full of grace and truth.

For the law was given by Moses, but grace and truth came by Jesus Christ.

No man hath seen God at any time; the only begotten Son, which is in the bosom of the Father, he hath declared him (John 1:1-5, 9-14, 17-18).

The grave was empty, and the Jewish authorities could not produce a body to disprove the claim that Jesus was alive from the dead. Scripture teaches that Jesus' followers shall share in His resurrection. When a person becomes a Christian he already experiences the life of the risen Jesus working in his own life. Christians can look forward with confidence to their own bodily resurrection into paradise. Believers must face physical death, for to each man is appointed once to die, but they are assured of a future with Christ in a new spiritual existence. The resurrection for all who have put their faith and trust in Jesus Christ is a resurrection of the complete person in a new and more wonderful body.

John's Gospel makes clear that Jesus' miracles were 'signs' He was the Messiah, signs that the new age of the Kingdom of God had really come. When the imprisoned John the Baptist had doubts and wanted to know if Jesus really was the Messiah, he was told of the miracles Jesus did and left to draw his own conclusions. By doing miracles Jesus was showing the people, all people, the Kingdom of God. He was giving examples of the fact that in the new age sin and death and sickness would be no more.

Jesus gave His disciples power to do miracles. They continued to heal in the power of Jesus after Pentecost, and miracles remained part of the experience of the early church, and even today many are claiming healings and miracles. One of the 'gifts of the Spirit' mentioned by Paul is the working of miracles, another of the gifts is healing. All glory goes to the one who heals and performs all miracles, who is always God Himself by His Spirit, never the Christian or the church (1 Cor. 12:3-11; see also Gal. 5:19-25).

Long before the time of Jesus, the prophet Jeremiah saw that men and women need to be completely remade from within if they are to have a renewed relationship with God (Jer. 31:31-34). In Jesus' discussion with the Jewish leader Nicodemus, He made the same point. Jesus said that only if a man be reborn in and with the Spirit of God could that man enter the kingdom of God (John 3:1-21). This fundamental change is God's healing miracle by the Spirit which occurs when a person becomes a Christian.

> Therefore if any man be in Christ, he is a new creature: old things are passed away; behold, all things are become new. And all things are of God, who hath reconciled us to himself by Jesus Christ, and hath given to us the ministry of reconciliation; To wit, that God was in Christ, reconciling the world unto himself, not imputing their trespasses unto them (2 Cor. 5:17-19).

Baptism is the outward sign of this new life. The new life is manifested by the indwelling Holy Spirit. The eternal life of God's Kingdom will be shared with others in the family of Jesus Christ and His Church. The eternal life of God's kingdom also will be inhabited by those earlier saints who were favoured by God for their righteousness in His eyes and the saints who looked forward to and trusted God's Word of the coming Messiah: 'And though after my skin worms destroy this body, yet in my flesh shall I see God' (Job 19:26).

Once reborn in Jesus we are assured by God that 'no weapon that is formed against thee shall proper' (Is. 54:17). Trust in Jesus for 'he was numbered with the transgressors; and he bare the sin of many, and made intercession for the transgressors' (Is. 53:12). Jesus 'was wounded for our transgressions, he was bruised for our iniquities: the chastisement of our peace was upon him; and with his stripes we are healed. All we like sheep have gone astray; we have turned every one to his own way; and the Lord hath laid on [Jesus] the iniquity of us all. ... Yet it pleased the Lord to bruise him; he hath put him to grief: when thou shalt make his soul an offering for sin, he shall see his seed, he shall prolong his days, and the pleasure of the Lord shall prosper in his hand' (Is. 53:5-6, 10).

The millennial kingdom of Christ will be a place where the resurrected saints reside in peace and wholeness:

The wilderness and the solitary place shall be glad for them; and the desert shall rejoice, and blossom as the rose. It shall blossom abundantly, and rejoice even with joy and singing: the glory of Lebanon shall be given unto it, the excellency of Carmel and Sharon, they shall see the glory of the Lord, and the excellency of our God.

Strengthen ye the weak hands, and confirm the feeble knees. Say to them that are of a fearful heart, Be strong, fear not: behold your God will come with vengeance, even God with a recompence: he will come and save you.

Then the eyes of the blind shall be opened, and the ears of the deaf shall be unstopped. Then shall the lame man leap as an hart [deer], and the tongue of the dumb sing: for in the wilderness shall waters break out, and streams in the desert. And the parched ground shall become a pool, and the thirsty land springs of water: in the habitation of dragons, where each lay, shall be grass with reeds and rushes.

And an highway shall be there, and a way, and it shall be called The way of holiness; the unclean shall not pass over it; but it shall be for those: the wayfaring men, though fools, shall not err therein. No lion shall be there, nor any ravenous beast shall go up thereon, it shall not be found there; but the redeemed shall walk there; And the ransomed of the Lord shall return, and come to Zion with songs and everlasting joy upon their heads: they shall obtain joy and gladness, and sorrow and sighing shall flee away (Is. 35).

Through our faith in the Risen Christ, the only begotten Son of God who died for our sins, we will be singing this song upon our resurrection:

And in that day thou shalt say, O Lord, I will praise thee: though thou wast angry with me, thine anger is turned away, and thou comfortedst me.

Behold, God is my salvation; I will trust, and not be afraid: for the Lord JEHOVAH is my strength and my song; he also is become my salvation.

Therefore with joy shall ye draw water out of the wells of salvation.

And in that day shall ye say, Praise the Lord, call upon his name, declare his doings among the people, make mention that his name is exalted.

Sing unto the Lord; for he hath done excellent things: this is known in all the earth.

Cry out and shout, thou inhabitant of Zion: for great is the Holy One of Israel in the midst of thee (Is. 12).

God promises each of us a place in the glorious Kingdom of God where there are no more tears and no more pain and joy is everlasting in the presence of the Father, Son and Holy Spirit. The decision for each of us is personal and should be made today, at this very moment: Trust the teaching of Jesus: be born again of water and of the Spirit by believing in the Risen Christ Jesus. (John 3:5). 'For God so loved the world, that he gave his only begotten Son, that whosoever believeth in him should not perish, but have everlasting life' (John 3:16). The gift is free from God (Rom. 5:15-16, 18).

Jesus is calling you by the Spirit of God. My prayer is that you listen to the Holy Spirit calling, calling you in your heart, and that you today answer by asking and believing that Jesus the Christ died for your sins and was risen from the grave to be your Saviour and Lord:

The word in nigh thee, even in thy mouth, and in thy heart: that is, the word of faith, which we preach;

That if thou shalt confess with thy mouth the Lord Jesus, and shalt believe in thine heart that God hath raised him from the dead, thou shalt be saved. For with the heart man believeth unto righteousness; and with the mouth confession is made unto salvation.

For the scripture saith, Whosoever believeth on him shall not be ashamed... For whosoever shall call upon the name of the Lord shall be saved (Rom. 10:8-11, 13).

SCRIPTURE INDEX

Christian Focus Publications publishes biblically-accurate books for adults and children. The books in the adult range are published in three imprints.

Christian Heritage contains classic writings from the past.

Christian Focus contains popular works including biographies, commentaries, doctrine, and Christian living.

Mentor focuses on books written at a level suitable for Bible College and seminary students, pastors, and others; the imprint includes commentaries, doctrinal studies, examination of current issues, and church history.

For a free catalogue of all our titles, please write to

Christian Focus Publications Ltd.,
Geanies House, Fearn, Tain,
Ross-shire, IV20 1TW, Great Britain

For details of our titles visit us on our web site

http://www.christianfocus.com